Becoming Human

Becoming Human

Fundamentals of Interreligious Education and
Didactics from a Muslim-Christian Perspective

Zekirija Sejdini, Martina Kraml and Matthias Scharer

PETER LANG
Oxford • Bern • Berlin • Bruxelles • New York • Wien

Bibliographic information published by Die Deutsche Nationalbibliothek.
Die Deutsche Nationalbibliothek lists this publication in the Deutsche National-
bibliografie; detailed bibliographic data is available on the Internet at
http://dnb.d-nb.de.

A catalogue record for this book is available from the British Library.

Library of Congress Control Number: 2020910606

Cover design: Peter Lang.

ISBN 978-1-78874-720-2 (print) • ISBN 978-1-78874-721-9 (ePDF)
ISBN 978-1-78874-722-6 (ePub) • ISBN 978-1-78874-723-3 (mobi)

© Peter Lang AG 2020

Published by Peter Lang Ltd, International Academic Publishers,
52 St Giles, Oxford, OX1 3LU, United Kingdom
oxford@peterlang.com, www.peterlang.com

Zekirija Sejdini, Martina Kraml and Matthias Scharer have asserted their right
under the Copyright, Designs and Patents Act, 1988, to be identified as Authors of
this Work.

© 2017 W. Kohlhammer GmbH, Stuttgart.

All rights reserved.
All parts of this publication are protected by copyright.
Any utilisation outside the strict limits of the copyright law, without
the permission of the publisher, is forbidden and liable to prosecution.
This applies in particular to reproductions, translations, microfilming,
and storage and processing in electronic retrieval systems.

This publication has been peer reviewed.

Contents

Foreword by the Publishers of the Series — vii

Introduction — 1

CHAPTER 1
Contexts We Move In — 25

CHAPTER 2
Anthropology – Theology – Education: Our Agreed-upon Foundations — 43

CHAPTER 3
Religious Pedagogy and Religious Didactics: How Do We Approach Them? — 79

CHAPTER 4
Possibility-Sensitive Religious Pedagogy and Religious Didactics — 111

CHAPTER 5
Possibility-Suitable Conceptualizations of Interreligious Educational Processes — 131

Epilogue — 149

Bibliography — 151

Foreword by the Publishers of the Series

Religious and cultural diversity is increasingly visible. This is resulting in important challenges that affect – in addition to politics, society and cultures – religions in particular. In the field of university education, particularly academic religious education, an adequate treatment of these challenges has so far only been possible to a limited extent, since, in the university landscape, research and teaching in the theological departments has often been concerned only with Christianity. This was the case for a long time in Innsbruck, until the study of Islamic Religious Education was established in the academic year 2013/2014 and the Institute for Islamic Theology and Religious Education was founded in 2017.

Since 2017, there has been close cooperation in research and teaching between the Institute for Islamic Theology and Religious Education and scholars of Catholic Religious Education. This cooperation includes, among other things, courses on religious didactics, internships and the study of interreligious teaching and learning processes in the context of schools and universities.

This research and collaboration needed an appropriate framework for presenting the results, but also for providing a platform for the publication and discussion of those results. Consequently, the German-language series 'Studies in Interreligious Religious Education/Studien zur Interreligiösen Religionspädagogik' (published by Kohlhammer) was launched. The book *Mensch werden. Grundlagen einer interreligiösen Religionspädagogik und –didaktik aus muslimisch-christlicher Perspektive*[1] is the first volume in the series. It deals with the basics of interreligious religious pedagogy and religious didactics. Subsequently, more volumes with different emphases have been published, such as, for example, the second volume in the series,

---

[1] Sejdini, Zekirija, Kraml, Martina, and Scharer, Matthias, *Mensch werden. Grundlagen einer interreligiösen Religionspädagogik und –didaktik aus muslimisch-christlicher Perspektive* (Studien zur Interreligiösen Religionspädagogik, Vol. 1). Stuttgart 2017.

entitled *Interreligiöse Bildungsprozesse. Empirische Einblicke in Schul- und Hochschulkontexte*.[2] The book you are reading is the translation of the first German-language volume.

This series could not have been established if we had not received various kinds of support from many people. Since it would be beyond the scope of this foreword to personally thank everyone, we would like to take this opportunity to single out our faculty teams in Islamic and Catholic Religious Education, the team of the research project 'Interreligious Education as a Contribution to a Pluralistic Society' and Matthias Scharer, who not only inspired us to create this series, but also participated in the writing of the first volume, for which we are thankful. A special thank goes to our project assistant Clemens Danzl, who managed and coordinated the first volume in the series in an exemplary manner and provided many ideas and suggestions. Special thanks also go to Jonas Kolb, who contributed significantly to the completion of the present English-language version of the first volume. Furthermore, we would like to thank Peter Lang for making the publication of the volume possible. Finally, we would like to give thanks to the 'Federal Ministry for Europe: Integration and Foreign Affairs' of the Republic of Austria for its financial support of the project.

Martina Kraml and Zekirija Sejdini
Innsbruck, January 2020

---

[2] Kraml, Martina, and Sejdini, Zekirija (eds.), *Interreligiöse Bildungsprozesse. Empirische Einblicke in Schul- und Hochschulkontexte* (Studien zur Interreligiösen Religionspädagogik, Vol. 2). Stuttgart 2018.

Introduction

Goals and Motivation of our Book

As religious pedagogues and religious didacts, we deal with (religious) educational processes. Current social and religious challenges, arising from heterogeneity and plurality, have prompted us to conceptualize an interreligious religious pedagogy, primarily from an Islamic-Catholic perspective.

Nowadays, Islam is frequently presented as a 'problematic religion,' Islamophobia characterizes our context, and 'national introversion'[1] endangers any sustainable model of Europe. In this context, theologians and religious pedagogues must exert themselves to help shape a plural future and to promote plurality-sensitive and socially (and religiously) inclusive development, particularly in the area of education.

In society and in education, a growing trend toward fear of plurality is discernible, and is, therefore, specifically addressed in this book. Wherever people are confronted with strangers, uncertainties and fears arise, as has occurred in response to expanding migration movements in recent times. Such uncertainties and fears are frequently politically fomented and distorted. There is usually a level of fear in encounters between people with different ideological and religious convictions. This also applies to Muslims and Christians in the European context. Religious plurality in Europe is increasingly perceived as a threat due to prevailing conflicts all over the world. On the other hand, in our opinion, perception and recognition of, as well as confrontation with, plurality 'at eye level' represent one of the

---

[1] Insam, Heribert, Lieber mutig statt ängstlich. In: *Tiroler Tageszeitung*, January 6, 2017, 4f.

most urgent challenges for education and, therefore, for an interreligious religious pedagogy and religious didactics.

We, as the authors of this book, not only want to present a suitable approach for dealing with plurality, but we also want to live that approach ourselves and, after multiple attempts, and the exchange of various ideas for this book, we decided to write the volume together, as a collective effort. One of our concerns was that what we consider important with regard to an interreligious religious pedagogy and religious didactics should also be visible in the premise, the range of themes discussed and the implementation. In the process of creating the book, we learned that co-writing requires considerably more effort than assembling individual texts. It also became clear to us that the texts we would have written individually would have had very different forms to a text written communally. During the co-writing process, a special style of writing developed that exhibits individual aspects of each of us, but nonetheless constitutes an independent 'organism' and reflects many shared experiences and countless discussions. This also led us not to describe the Christian and the Muslim perspectives side by side, or one after the other, but rather to link them to each other, and thus, as Muslims and Christians, to consider the themes that we addressed together without disregarding our respective differences.

Another concern of this book is to shed light on the subject of interreligious religious pedagogy and religious didactics at the level of the human and professional encounter. Therefore, we focus not on the explicit reception of extensive interreligious publications and concepts, but rather on the questions and problems that move us in our concrete, collective interreligious work and reveal themselves in the process of rapprochement; the questions and problems that have arisen and played out in the society in which we live and continue to do so. This does not mean that previous publications and conceptions were not received and appreciated, but rather that we have chosen a different focus.

In this sense, it is the basics of an interreligious religious pedagogy and religious didactics that the three of us collectively reflect on, take into consideration, and engage with from an inner religious pedagogical theological perspective. In this process, it was always important to us to seek and find God, not only within and among ourselves or in our own religion or denomination, but also with and among our neighbors and friends.² Since the two fields – religious didactics and religious pedagogy – are closely linked to one another, we decided to discuss both religious pedagogy and religious didactics. Here, we understand religious pedagogy and religious didactics as theological sciences, which are aligned – in the case of religious pedagogy – with educational processes and – in the case of religious didactics – with teaching and learning processes in institutions.

Concrete methodological instructions are not a central focus of this volume. Instead, the book offers a foundation, background information and conceptual considerations. It is important for us to hold on to the idea that interreligious religious pedagogy and religious didactics are not ends in themselves, but rather serve to help learners and are thus geared toward the 'good life' for all. Thus, we hope that this volume can contribute to interreligious solidarity.

The guiding principles are awareness of the significance of the biography of the person; paying attention to interaction and communication; consideration of the context that surrounds us; and what is at stake in each case. Therefore, we begin by offering our own biographical narratives as examples. In Chapter 1, we examine the current context, which conditions us. In Chapter 2, we discuss the anthropological, theological and educational theoretical foundations of interreligious religious pedagogy and religious didactics, which are based on the example of Christianity and Islam. Chapter 3 clarifies the basics of the Innsbruck religious pedagogy and religious didactics from a Christian and Muslim point of view. This is further developed in the empirically oriented second volume of this series, entitled *Interreligiöse Bildungsprozesse. Empirische Einblicke in Schul- und Hochschulkontexte*.³ In Chapter 4, we lay the foundation for a possibility-suitable and contingency-sensitive understanding of interreligious religious pedagogy and religious didactics. Chapter 5 develops – only provisionally conclusive – guidelines for and the main features of such as religious pedagogy and religious didactics.

---

2   See Largen Johnson, Kristin, *Finding God Among Our Neighbours. An Interfaith Systematic Theology*. Minneapolis, MN 2013.
3   Kraml and Sejdini (eds.), *Interreligiöse Bildungsprozesse*.

Genesis of our Interreligious Collaboration

In the winter semester of 2013/2014, a bachelor's degree program in Islamic Religious Education and a professorship of the same name were established in the School of Education at the University of Innsbruck. Since then, there has been intensive collaboration between the Islamic and Catholic branches of religious pedagogy in research and teaching.

This book is concerned with the commonalities of these branches of study. The reflections on an interreligious religious pedagogy and religious didactics presented in this book emerged from an intensive and lengthy process of encounters and reflection.

When we speak of interreligious religious pedagogy in this book, we are aware that we are developing the idea exclusively as Islamic and Catholic religious pedagogues and that the point of view of Judaism, our sister religion, as well as the points of view of other religious communities, which have the right to inclusion in Austria's schools and educational institutions, are missing. In this respect, we do not see our work as a complete conception of an interreligious religious pedagogy, but rather as an example of the way in which it could emerge.

As we have already mentioned, we do not aspire to present a systematic description of other publications or to examine documents of religious communities, as other authors have already written extensively on this matter.[4] Instead, the purpose of this publication is to foreground the people, the process and the dynamics of encounters in the development of

---

4 See, especially, Leimgruber, Stephan, *Interreligiöses Lernen*. Munich 2007; Schambeck, Mirjam, *Interreligiöse Kompetenz. Basiswissen für Studium, Ausbildung und Beruf*. Göttingen 2013; Schweitzer, Friedrich, *Interreligiöse Bildung. Religiöse Vielfalt als religionspädagogische Herausforderung und Chance*. Munich 2014; Müller, Rabeya, Islamische Perspektiven zum interreligiösen Lernen: Wie 'inter-' ist der Islam? In: Schreiner, Peter (ed.), *Handbuch interreligiöses Lernen*. Gütersloh 2005, 142–149; Sejdini, Zekirija, Interreligiöser Dialog aus muslimischer Perspektive. In: Gmainer-Pranz, Franz, Ingruber, Astrit, and Ladstätter, Markus (eds.), '... *mit Klugheit und Liebe'. Dokumentation der Tagung zur Förderung des interreligiösen Dialogs 2012–2015*. Linz 2017, 241–251.

religious pedagogical and religious didactic concepts. With this in mind, we begin the book with the religious pedagogical significance of narrations, or *stories*, after which we present our own biographical narratives as examples.

Our Stories

Toward a Religious Pedagogical Signification of Stories[5]

People's life and faith stories and the development of their thinking and judgment have gained importance in German-language religious pedagogy.[6] This is not only due to the fact that – in keeping with religious pedagogical standards – people are taken seriously, in order to perform didactically 'correctly.' Rather, human beings, as subjects, as well as through their interactional references, are granted an independent and inviolable dignity that renders them and their lives the source of theological and religious pedagogical insights and, therefore, irreplaceable.

People, as individuals and subjects in relation to one another and to a final cause, reveal, in their *stories*, who they are, what being human, in all its ambivalence, means (anthropological dignity) and ultimately also a trace of what God's action[7] through man or woman means and how, at the same

---

5   We use here the English term *story*, because there has been a rapid increase in the religious pedagogical use of (biographical) narrations and storytelling in American Religious Pedagogy in recent years. Numerous publications focus on storytelling and narrations or narration research. See, among others, Egan, Kieran, *Teaching as story telling. An alternative approach to teaching and the curriculum*. Chicago 1989; Ellis, Gail, and Brewster, Jean, *Tell it again! – The new storytelling handbook for primary teachers*. Harlow 2002.

6   See Pirker, Viera, Lernen mit der eigenen Biografie in der Religionslehrerbildung. Theoretische Aspekte. In: *Religionspädagogische Beiträge. Zeitschrift der Arbeitsgemeinschaft Katholische Religionspädagogik und Katechetik* (2016) 74, 56–67.

7   See Siebenrock, Roman A. (ed.), *Handeln Gottes. Beiträge zur aktuellen Debatte*. Freiburg i. Br. 2014.

time, it remains mysteriously concealed from us (theological dignity). In this respect, the *stories*, in our view, are a fitting object of anthropological, theological and religious pedagogical research, which demands appropriate methodological competence and diligence. Anyone who has learned to approach with scientific honesty and awe the fragmentary experiences of life and faith, which reveal themselves in human narratives, also gains the competence in applying religious pedagogy in everyday life that is necessary to learn, theologically and religious pedagogically, from the *stories* of children, adolescents and adults.

Our own biographical narratives are not intended as self-presentations. On the one hand, they serve to render us tangible as people whose work focuses on religion and theology or religious pedagogy. On the other hand, they document our understanding of religious doctrine, in which, as authors, we take ourselves seriously and due to which we value ourselves as people with our very different lives, beliefs and narratives. This illustrates, on a scientific theoretical level, that religious pedagogy and religious didactics would be almost inconceivable without empirical insights. Therefore, empirical, particularly qualitative empirical, research also belongs to the standard of interreligious religious pedagogy.

Despite the need for empirical insight, it is clear that it is difficult to arrive at empirical results, especially for practicing religious pedagogues. As a result of close collaboration with so-called practitioners, however, we have arrived at the conviction that the customary separation between researchers and practitioners (at least in the context of religious pedagogy) is not appropriate; instead, we must strive to make the interdependence of roles clear. The insights that religious pedagogues gain from their daily dealings with people in the various fields of religious pedagogy are therefore not devoid of theory. On the one hand, every person possesses a wealth of implicit and explicit theories (ideas) of varying complexity. On the other hand, in practice, it is important for people to become aware of the ideas or concepts that shape their religious pedagogical action and inaction. Thus, in our biographical narratives, we wish to share aspects of our human, religious, theological and religious pedagogical views that will encourage interested readers to become aware of their own formative conceptions.[8]

Anyone who takes his or her own life and faith history seriously will do this in relation to others, be they children, adults or the elderly. The sensorium of *awareness*, the attentive and empathetic awareness of other people, increases with self-awareness. Awareness of self and others depends on taking the 'empirical view,' derived from the concrete processes of everyday life situations and experiences. This awareness can be practiced day by day through small examples and reflected upon scientifically, until it becomes an attitude in the professional practice of religious pedagogy and religious didactics.

Our Own Biographical Narratives

Through our biographical self-narratives, we want to give insights into our life paths, so that you can get an idea of who we are and how the events of our lives have influenced the development of our ideas. We also want to connect with you as a reader and encourage you to become aware of your own history, attitudes, insights and questions regarding Muslim–Christian religious pedagogy and religious didactics.

Martina Kraml

I, Martina Kraml, was born in 1956 on a small farm. My father returned from the war disabled by injuries and my mother was often sick, so my everyday life – outside of school – was very much determined by participation in farm work. I often experienced first-hand the extent to which we, as farmers, were affected by the rigors of weather or other inconveniences: The illness of one cow sometimes threatened our existence.

---

[8] For critical, contingency-sensitive references to biographical narratives, see, in particular, Nassehi, Armin, and Saake, Irmhild, Kontingenz: Methodisch verhindert oder beobachtet? In: *Zeitschrift für Soziologie* (2002) 1, 66–86.

Life in my childhood home was – because of the uncertainties and insecurities of everyday life, it seems to me – very much determined by the Catholic religion and ecclesiasticism, which offered support, confidence, security and hope. Furthermore, for my father, observance of the norms and the fulfillment of daily individual and communal ecclesiastical practice were essential, while my mother was very much influenced by prayer and her inner relationship with God. As a child, I soon noticed the inherent contradictions and tensions of faith and religion in the individual and in the parish context: I observed early on how much the positive or negative attitude of the church and its officials influenced people's chances of advancement and the social differences between people.

Over the course of the educational campaign of the 1960s, an academic high school (*Gymnasium*) was built in a neighboring village. The fourth-grade director convinced my father that I should attend this academic high school. This was not the normal path at the time for a young girl. I still remember that my father was visited by relatives who had a serious talk with him, arguing that it would be better to send a daughter to a home economics school than to an academic high school, because this would be a better preparation for marriage.

The academic high school was a particularly exciting place for me. Young teachers came from outside the area, bringing new ideas and approaches. There was greater cultural openness at the school, which caused the inhabitants and politicians of the villages to feel skeptical and uneasy. It struck me that the Church always adopts a conservative stance on themes and in discussions. Our German and history teacher, our mathematics teacher and a few others taught me new ideological opinions, approaches to literature, and unconventional perspectives. Nevertheless, religion was my favorite subject, but I rarely agreed with the religion teachers we had. I sensed the great tension between what seemed to me to be new, 'free' thinking and the religious realm, which was characterized by many norms and taboos. This tension interested me, because I was used to frequent and open debates at home. In religion class, I had many questions, to which I sought answers. That is how I began studying theology. However, due to a range of circumstances, after graduation I attended the Pedagogical Academy, as it was then called, and was trained as an elementary school teacher. For three years, I taught first and second grades in a small village. Only when my brother had grown older and could support my parents in the management of the farm did I pursue my desire to study.

Through the study of theology and, later, philosophy – and theoretical discussions in particular – a broader perspective on religion and faith opened up to me, with both fields of study having a stimulating effect on one another. I was also drawn, through my experiences as an elementary school teacher, in action-theoretical, linguistic-philosophical, and hence philosophical-pragmatic directions in theology and philosophy.

After having worked as a teacher and raised my children, I decided to write a dissertation on catechetics/religious pedagogy with a focus on Eucharistic catechesis. I dealt with the theoretical question of the role of theology as an extension of naturalistic and cultural viewpoints. I elucidated this using the example of the Eucharistic catechesis and argued for a broadening of the understanding of the Eucharistic catechetical toward a Eucharistic culture of life. In the process, I took into consideration approaches from the social sciences and the humanities. I described my own scientific and methodological process of cognition in this work. From a theological perspective, it criticized approaches to action theory that neglected the experience of passivity, ambivalences and ambiguities, placing the research in the context of the research program 'Communicative Theology' and the Theological Research Center 'Religion–Violence–Communication–World Order.' Theoretical and methodological approaches to the topic of contingency that determined my later research can be recognized here for the first time.

In 2001, I started working at the Department of Catechetics/Religious Pedagogy of the Faculty of Catholic Theology in Innsbruck. I was an assistant to Matthias Scharer for more than 10 years. At first, the main focus of my work was more on questions of theological criteriology, the further development of communicative theology and theological hermeneutics in catechetics/religious pedagogy. Through the paradigms of theme-centered interaction and communicative theology established in the faculties, multiperspectivity and process orientation, as well as sensitivity to the theological perspective, became part of my scientific training. I also became aware of the importance of paying attention to difference. Against the background of my educational and scientific formation, which was more oriented toward the homologous and the tabooing of negation,[9] difference orientation resulted in an attitude change with regard to the conception and evaluation of differences and conflicts, as well as the appreciation of the heterogeneous.

In 2007, my interreligious commitment began as part of an initiative of the Faculty of Catholic Theology in Innsbruck. It was very important to me that the 3rd Congress of Communicative Theology should not take place at the Theological Faculty or at the University of Innsbruck, but rather out in the world, where Muslims, Christians and secular people live their everyday lives. We therefore decided to hold the congress in Telfs. In keeping with the desire to learn how we live out in the world, we held an empirically oriented conference in January 2008, that is, three months before the congress. This sensitized us to living together, and the challenges and tensions on the ground.

This congress and subsequent, related events marked the birth of interreligious engagement in the Communicative Theology research program and the Institute of Practical Theology, as well as my personal involvement. The establishment of the Islamic Religious Education program also initiated the beginning of cooperation between the Institute of Practical Theology and the Islamic Religious Education program. I was particularly inspired by the interreligious work. It was in this area that political awareness and the pursuit of change to achieve a better life for all – both of which have always been central to me – could be combined with scientific activity. There was the possibility that something new could emerge, and I was convinced that a good future for our country depended on whether

---

[9] 'Homologue' refers to conceptions of a similar world, similar thinking and similar convictions. Irmhild Saake speaks of 'homology acceptance,' which determines communication and interaction with the others. Stability, continuity and coherence play an important role in this context. Negations are rejected. See Saake, Irmhild, Selbstbeschreibungen als Weltbeschreibungen. Die Homologie-Annahme revisited. In: *Sociologia Internationalis. Europäische Zeitschrift für Kulturforschung* (2005) 1/2, 99–139, 107.

and to what extent religions could communicate. I also observed the same desire for upheaval in others, for example, in the staff members in the Islamic and Catholic Religious Education Departments, as well as the practical teachers. I am deeply convinced that a good future can only be achieved if the religions seek to cooperate and find common ground. In side-by-side exclusivity, there can be no good life. One day we will have to answer to God for the pictures we continue to hand down of him, especially the pictures we pass on to children.

Another significant and sustained phase in my life was my collaboration with Christin Münz, a colleague with whom I worked for years as part of Qualitas, a social science networking group. Unfortunately, Christin Münz died very early from a serious chronic illness. Her life themes were influenced by the illness. In many conversations, in the group as well as between the two of us, we talked about the topic of contingency, which we discuss in Chapter 4 in the context of interreligious religious pedagogy and religious didactics. We discussed the theses of Richard Rorty, the empirical findings regarding the central question of my post-doctoral thesis, and the modeling of the 'space of possibilities' in the sense of the space of contingency. I was particularly interested in the question of contingency sensitivity in teaching, science and research. After reading texts by Armin Nassehi and Irmhild Saake,[10] I became aware of numerous contingency invisibilization techniques – in other words, the invisibilization or concealment of contingency in scientific disciplines, methodologies and methods. Triggered by collective discussions, I entered a self-critical phase, which raised questions about problematic contingency-invisibilizing contents and strategies of our own religious didactic and communicative theological models. It became clear to me that talking about contingency sensitivity is one thing and cultivating it – in dealing with one's own models – is another. During that time, I dealt intensively with the question of how much self-criticism and restraint it takes not to destructure one's own speech regarding contingency sensitivity.

---

10   See Nassehi and Saake, Kontingenz, 66–86; Saake, Selbstbeschreibungen als Weltbeschreibungen, 99–139.

Thereafter, with a view to fostering Muslim–Christian cooperation, I hoped to ensure that my Muslim colleagues could develop authentically and thought that we Christians should be cautious in promoting our own models. In light of the approaches of other religions, all of our European models of thought, Christian or non-Christian, must be put to the test again and thoroughly reconsidered. Everyone who enters a community, in particular the scientific community, as an individual or collectively, changes it and the others in the community. Seeing these changes, and allowing oneself be changed, seems to me to be the challenge of interreligious religious didactics.

In religious contexts in particular, the question of truth is constantly being shifted and is quickly thematized, sometimes too quickly and too often. In the process, certainty and possible uncertainty play a significant role. Recently, a student referred to Church documents in his argument in support of them, insisting, on the basis of the documents, that one is definitely 'on the safe side.' I have never forgotten this. It gave rise to the following questions in me: Can the Church, Church documents or holy scriptures really provide us with security in our everyday action and faith in the world? Is it not the insecurity and uncertainty in the condition of plurality that we have to come to terms with? Furthermore, we cannot pass on security in a static sense. The task is rather to guide people through the current challenges so that they can find an appropriate path through all the imponderables and uncertainties. I would like to conclude my biographical narration with a quotation from Timon Beyes' dissertation, which currently serves as a guiding motto for me:

> Even when we leave aside the inexhaustible confusion of opinions among philosophers, those universal and seemingly endless arguments about the cognizance of things, those incessant quarrels and disagreements (for it may well be undisputed that even those inherently skillful scholars are not in agreement about anything, not even over the fact that the sky is above our heads ...) – even if, out of the confusion into which our own judgment plunges us, it is easy to see that it stands on very shaky ground.[11]

---

11 De Montaigne, Michel, *Essais*. Cited in Beyes, Timon Paul, *Kontingenz und Management*. St Gallen 2002, 6.

Introduction

Matthias Scharer

I, Matthias Scharer, am the oldest of us three authors (born in 1946). I am a Catholic Christian, shaped by the post-war Catholic folk-church milieu. I grew up in a middle-sized town in Austria, on a simple, small-scale farm. The simple living conditions that I experienced during my childhood help me to this day in encounters with people in societies and cultures that are not blessed with the wealth of Europe or North America. Among Latin Americans, Indians or Africans, I feel good and accepted. I am also grateful to the poor living conditions of my childhood, as a result of which I did not have to attend the church boarding school run by the local pastor. This would have been opposed by my father, who was skeptical of the church, which led to frequent disputes over religion with my mother, who was pious and faithful to the church.

An academic high school had recently been built in my district, so I was able to go from middle school to academic high school. In relation to the formation of my view of mankind, daily discussions with classmates during the train journeys to school may have had a greater influence on me than school itself. Probably in advance of the movement of 1968, with its religious and socio-critical concerns, I read critics of religion, such as Nietzsche, Freud, and Feuerbach, among others, with enthusiasm. A religion teacher with a very open theology (he was writing his theological dissertation) stimulated my critical search. A passionate history teacher, prompted by our discussions of political issues, encouraged us to read the newspapers daily, which triggered intense political debates among us students during the train rides to and from school. During my time in high school, I worked on a critical student magazine, which made me want to become a journalist. With this goal in mind, after I had completed school and military service (which was still obligatory at the time), I began to study German literature and history.

It was my engagement with the community at my Catholic university that first gave me the idea that I could combine the study of history with theology. At that time, there were roughly 20 of us so-called lay theologians, compared to approximately 800 clerics, who were studying at the Theological Faculty of Salzburg. I was the only one who had no past experience with the Church, in the sense that I had not attended a church boarding school or ecclesiastic seminary, which has made it much easier for me to deal with church authorities. I confront the clergy with our common dignity as human beings and avoid the use of honorary titles for church officials.

My studies in the fields of theology and history frequently presented me, as a student, with a dichotomy: In the study of history, I learned to treat sources in a critical and scientific manner. In the study of theology, which was still partly influenced by neo-scholasticism at that time, sources on faith were dealt with in an ideologizing manner, which was considered unscientific by historians. Biblical texts were used to support a 'final,' doctrinal system called 'faith of the Church,' which was purportedly valid for all time. In order to view things from an alternative perspective, we formed theological 'self-help groups,' in which we dealt with the texts of the Second Vatican Council and theologians who were being discussed at that time, such as Küng, Schillebeeckx, Schoonenberg, and Rahner, among others. In addition to this, these groups had a political commitment, which was partly fueled by Marxist ideas. In particular, the dialogue between Christianity and Marxism was a defining concern for me. In the critical year 1966/1967, I was the top student in the university community and thus decidedly involved in the student movement that was critical of society and the Church. We rejected the involvement of the Americans in the Vietnam War, as well as the military chaplaincy of the Christian churches. My first connections with the emerging liberation theology of Latin America, with which I later became more deeply acquainted through longer encounters with its founder Gustavo Gutierrez and other liberation theologians during several Latin American sojourns, deeply influenced my perspective on the theological debate: How can we, in the face of deadly poverty, into which a large percentage of human beings are born, speak in good conscience of a liberating and loving God?

My encounter with contemplative movements, particularly the *zazen*, which stems from Buddhism, and which I practiced for decades, promoted the mystical approach to life and faith. Through the daily practice of inhaling and exhaling, coupled with letting go of all concrete ideas about God and the world, my understanding of God widened. Denominational and religious spiritual diversity resulted in a decrease in the theological ecclesiastical fear of losing one's own religion, beliefs or spirituality. I felt then and increasingly feel now that the denominational plurality in Christianity and the diversity of religions are gifts that enrich me as a searching and believing person. The balance of mysticism and politics that has to be achieved over and over again continues to define my theological search as a Catholic Christian.

Very early on, and without any religious pedagogical training, I stumbled into religion class as a young student. Due to the dearth of religion teachers in the 1960s, when the priests largely withdrew from teaching religion, I began, around the time I switched to theology studies, to work as a religion teacher, initially in an elementary school, later in a main school (*Hauptschule*) and a polytechnic school, and lastly – still without a completed degree in Catholic religious pedagogy – in an academic high school. Through religious education, and in close cooperation with, above all, 'left-wing' teachers from other disciplines, many of us working students, in the face of great resistance from the school management and our established colleagues, tried to change the severely rigorous and, in many areas, inhumane school. The conversation regarding Reformed Education shaped our ideas of an open school, in which the students, as human beings, and not as subjects, should be the focus of the educational effort. In spite of all the differentiation in the subsequent religious pedagogical studies and research, the search for the existential concerns of children, adolescents, and adults remains a concern of primary importance in my educational work. Furthermore, this people-centeredness always makes me skeptical of pedagogical-didactic paradigms, which focus solely on measurable goals and comparable competences.

Through close cooperation with the religious pedagogue in Graz, Albert Höfer, with whom I had already written a textbook for the polytechnic course, and through relevant training in gestalt pedagogy, I also learned to appreciate other reformed pedagogical approaches such as those of Freinet or Montessori, which still influence my didactic thinking and actions today. Elements of 'curricular didactics,' which terminologically guided the post-conciliar decision of the Würzburg Synod on Religious Instruction and which initiated the change from content/substance concentration to learning target orientation, contributed to a clear structuring of the didactic endeavor. The four-step curriculum of planning, teaching, evaluating and revising supported us students in the years during which we regularly prepared, as a team, religion instruction at different schools, and evaluated and revised it after class.

The decision to leave school and begin a career in church management and adult education was not an easy one for me. At first, between the ages of 26 and 30, frequently overburdened as Secretary General of the Catholic Action, I led a church 'operation' with approximately 60 employees and considerable budgetary responsibility. During this time, inwardly focused personnel guidance and outwardly focused church social engagement, complemented by conceptual developments and practice in adult education, were part of the everyday challenges. I also used this time to gain further relevant education and training in management, human resources management and group dynamics, which benefitted me greatly when carrying out leadership tasks at the university later.

At the age of 30, I returned to religious education. In addition to teaching, I was asked to participate in the newly established Religious Pedagogical Institute for Teacher Education, where I eventually became responsible for the area of higher education. In addition, there were teaching assignments at the university and a newly emerging interest in scientific research. Inspired by the religious pedagogue Albert Biesinger, I finally wrote a dissertation and, at the age of 40, completed my doctoral studies. My publications and additional training in psychological, group-pedagogical, and therapeutic approaches motivated the appointment committee of the Catholic-Theological University of Linz to propose that I be appointed to the professorship for Catechetics/Religious Pedagogy and Pedagogy. For exactly 10 years to the day, I was a professor – and, for the last two years, the first non-priest rector – in this institution, which had become the Catholic Private University of Linz. During my time in Linz, there was already close cooperation with colleagues studying biblical, systematic and philosophical subjects within and outside the faculty. I began to work on a kairology and criteriology of religious pedagogy, which, on the one hand, is closely linked to human scientific insights, in particular the psychology and sociology of religion, and, on the other hand, can be regarded as a situational

Introduction

fundamental theology. The theological perspective of religious pedagogical theory and practice are still very important to me today.

I went from Linz to the University of Innsbruck, where I was able to work as a religious pedagogue for more than 18 years with an excellent staff and where we developed, among other things, the Innsbruck model for religious teacher education. The stance and method of what Ruth C. Cohn calls 'theme-centered interaction' (TCI), which will be discussed in this book, has had a decisive influence on my understanding of people and the world. I encountered it for the first time in the 1980s, and trained people in this method for about 20 years as a graduate student at the Ruth Cohn Institute International. Building on this concept and in conjunction with a conciliar theology and liberation theological influences, I worked for decades with many other theologians on the concept of an interdisciplinary and international 'Communicative Theology.' This is not concerned with the question of how theology or faith can be communicated; but rather places revelation and faith occurrences, as communicative events, at the center of theological reflections.

The Muslim–Christian conversation, which inspired the Innsbruck concept of an interreligious religious teacher training program, arose from Communicative Theology, initially originating on the Catholic side. Despite my many years of experience working in Muslim–Christian teacher training, I have an increasing number of critical questions about whether the concept of the interreligious encounter, which was designed theologically on the basis of an expansion of the theological sites of cognizance to so-called *loci alieni*, does justice to the Muslim–Christian encounter, as we have understood and facilitated it for several years in the area of religious pedagogy in Innsbruck. The experiences in interreligious groups that I have had in recent years, particularly in India, tend instead to bring me back to the TCI concept, with its humanistic anthropology and its 'art of group leadership.' On that basis, in living processes with people of different religions and worldviews, I attempt to become aware of and holistically process those generative themes and issues that move people in the here and now, without excluding questions from the different traditions to which the participants belong. In order to gain religious pedagogical insights from this, I still keep on oscillating between the three levels of theologizing that we developed in Communicative Theology, which will be presented in the relevant section.

Against the background of my human, scientific-theological and religious-pedagogical inquiries, which I have briefly outlined here, as the elder in our team of three, I openly embark on a Muslim–Christian encounter and learning process from which I have yet to finish learning.

Zekirija Sejdini

Although I, Zekirija Sejdini, was born in 1972 in Macedonia, the first life experiences I remember took place in Germany, where we emigrated with my mother before the end of my first year. We had followed my father, who arrived in Germany a year earlier as a laborer from Yugoslavia. Despite the fact that my German environment was not foreign to me, since I had known no other, it was always clear to me that as ethnic Albanian Muslims from Yugoslavia we were different from the native Germans. From our eating habits to our dress codes, it became clear to me very early that an important reason for my and our otherness was our religious affiliation. Not infrequently, that otherness led to me not being allowed to do things that were done as a matter of course by non-Muslim students. My father, who had come to Germany in the early 1970s with the intention of staying for a few months to earn money and then return, was an avowing and practicing Muslim. He had managed to become so self-taught in religion that, despite his lack of official training and in addition to his job as a locksmith, he worked voluntarily and passionately as an imam in a mosque in our village, Friedrichsfeld on the Lower Rhine. Through my father's volunteer work as an imam and his tireless commitment to the religious education of children and adolescents, I not only had a strong religious socialization, but also, at a very early age, acquired religious knowledge at the request of my father. Although he was enthusiastic about any kind of knowledge or science and had a great respect for educated people, his passion was Islamic theology. His greatest wish and dream was that one of his sons would graduate in Islamic theology and work as a scholar. So it was clear even before my first day at school that I would study Islamic theology. When my older brother managed to persuade my father to allow him not to study Islamic theology, my fate was 'sealed.' The attempt to produce an Islamic clergyman in our family would be sure to succeed this time.

It was decided very early what I should study and what activity I should undertake after my studies and I was educated accordingly. That is why I learned Arabic before I had even entered elementary school. After finishing elementary school and the fifth year at main school, I had to return to Macedonia with my mother for family reasons, which abruptly disconnected me from the German environment to which I was accustomed. I had to find my way in a new environment that was very foreign to the German environment in every respect.

This fundamental change, in the absence of my father, was a huge challenge for me. I had to learn three completely foreign languages – including the language of instruction – and come to terms with the fact that it was not uncommon in my new environment for students to be beaten by their teachers. Although, to the astonishment of many, I finished my first school year in Macedonia with honors, with the support of my older brother, the initial culture shock marked me deeply. In addition to the school experience, which was exhausting in the beginning, I tried, at the request of my father, to learn the Qur'an by heart with a recognized imam. Unlike my father, this idea did not inspire me at that time. Although I loved theologizing and Qur'an recitation very much, I did not really enjoy memorizing it. I memorized several hundred pages of the Qur'an, but this was not enough to fulfill my father's wish. This pressing desire of my father's that I memorize the entire Qur'an (which would have been of great benefit to me in my present activity) was an important turning point in my beliefs. By trying to memorize the entire Qur'an as a child, I lost the desire that I had previously had regarding theology. As a result, I came to believe that religion was an obstacle that kept me from being what I wanted to be in those days: a child, like any other child, who did not spend hours after school being forced to learn Qur'an by heart, instead of playing with other children on the street. This was the first break with my naive childlike beliefs. I still felt the limits set in the name of religion before, but never again with that intensity.

This event also marked the beginning of my critical confrontation with my religion and the emergence of my first doubts about the correctness of my chosen field of study. But my father's desire and the pressure I felt were too great to allow me to envisage an alternative. After completing my compulsory education, I studied for four years at the Islamic Secondary School in Skopje, the capital of Macedonia, and then in Pristina, the capital of Kosovo. The school in Skopje, which is comparable to a seminary, was a boarding school. Attending this secondary school, which was then the best in the country, brought an end to my naïve ideas about faith and represented my first important step toward independent thinking. This was not because of the teachers, who were well educated in classical subjects and inspired us to think critically, but rather because the discrepancy between Islam as it was lived and as it was preached was very evident in the behavior of 'highly respected professors,' as they were then considered.

In addition, the rules of the boarding school, which had no particular pedagogical basis, further complicated the lives and studies of all pupils. The excessive pressure of the rules replaced religion. The educator, who recorded our concrete offenses and uttered and executed our punishments, took on the role of God himself. It was our good fortune that there were no physical punishments, unlike in other schools, where violence was common. I rebelled against the rules of the boarding school, so I had to leave school for disciplinary reasons after three years as an excellent pupil. Thereafter, I attended an Islamic secondary school in Pristina that was not nearly as strict as the one in Skopje and there I was able to rehabilitate myself in every way and reconcile myself with my religion.

My studies at al-Azhar University in Cairo – which was renowned among Macedonian Muslims – were just as planned as my previous education had been. It was common practice for Muslims in Macedonia to attend this university to get a degree in theology. In Cairo, a new life began for me. After several years of being under total control, as an 18-year-old I was completely free. On another continent and in one of the largest cities in the world, I was on my own. That was a completely different feeling. But maybe it was too much freedom for me all at once. I realized on my first visit to al-Azhar University in the Hussain district that the university had its best years behind it and could not be an appropriate place to study. Moreover, the city of Cairo was much more attractive than the university, which made studying even more difficult. The reputation of al-Azhar University was so poor that most foreign students were reluctant to admit that they were studying at there. Often they even stated that they were studying at other, more prestigious universities.

After two years of language study and several other courses, I decided, on the advice of a colleague, to continue studying in Turkey. I was not very enthusiastic about studying in Turkey, as it was not common practice to study theology in Turkey, and I had not heard good things about Turkish theological faculties. But I wanted to complete my studies. This was my only motivation for continuing my studies in Turkey. In Istanbul, where I wished to continue my studies, I was pleasantly surprised. The theological faculty at Marmara University in Istanbul, where I began studying, offered a very good mix of Orient and Occident. We had the opportunity to take classical Islamic and human science subjects, which made my studies more interesting. After completing my five-year bachelor's degree program, I began my two-year master's program at the same university. Since I had opted for philosophy, I chose the conflict between philosophical hermeneutics as the topic of my master's thesis. My decision to engage with hermeneutics paved the way for me to go to Germany. I decided to travel to Heidelberg to study hermeneutics 'in situ' and to attend Gadamer's lectures.

After a one-year stay in Heidelberg, I completed my master's thesis on the philosophical foundations of hermeneutics and began to write my dissertation at the University of Heidelberg. Before I went to Germany, my father had died unexpectedly at only 61. Unfortunately, he did not live long enough to see me studying and graduating in Germany, which he could hardly wait for. His death was the most dramatic experience of my life. I never thought that his demise would have caused me so much pain.

After his death, my family lost its financial security. So I had to find a job to finance my Ph.D. In addition to pursuing my doctorate, I began working as a representative and coordinator for interreligious dialogue at a mosque in Stuttgart. I also availed of the opportunity to take on a teaching role at the Protestant University of Applied Sciences in Ludwigsburg. Shortly thereafter, I got married and continued my work as a coordinator at the mosque in Stuttgart.

Toward the end of 2004, I received an invitation from a friend to come to Vienna to work at the Islamic Religious Education Academy (IRPA). I gratefully accepted, as there were no opportunities in Germany for similar work. In Austria, I worked for two years as a department head of teaching at the Islamic Religious Education Academy. Afterwards, I moved to the school office of the Islamic Religious Community in Austria. I worked there for several years as a subject inspector, first for the general compulsory schools and then for the general education schools. During this time, I became deputy head of the Islamic Religious Education Bureau in Austria. In 2011, following the election of the Islamic Religious Community in Austria, I was given several duties in the religious community. In 2013, the opportunity arose to teach several courses at the University of Innsbruck as a lecturer, which led to my first encounters with the city and university, and my co-authors Martina and Matthias. I finally applied for the professorship for Islamic Religious Education at the University of Innsbruck and was given the position on January 1, 2014. Since then, I have been in Innsbruck with my family, enjoying interreligious cooperation with my Catholic colleagues.

Consequences for an Interreligious Religious Pedagogy and Religious Didactics

The interreligious religious pedagogy and religious didactics outlined by us in this volume are based on encounters. According to our experiences, such encounters are necessary in order to be able to perceive, and thereby render tangible, oneself and others as human beings with existential concerns. Out of these encounters, relationships can develop, which can enable the human being to reveal him- or herself in his or her vulnerability. The biographical narrative, which also discloses the background of the religious pedagogical approaches, enables such encounters, be they on a physical or a literary level. Whether and how biographical narratives are allotted space determines the quality of the religious pedagogical and religious didactic reflections. It is also important to take seriously the theologically based human dignity of the subjects, whether they are children, adolescents or adults. At the same time, biographical narratives should not be read naively in terms of scientific theory and practice. They are not descriptions of reality, but rather perspectives and points of view – in this case, first-person perspectives of their specific contexts.

CHAPTER I

Contexts We Move In

According to the religious pedagogical and religious didactic concept to which we feel committed, religious pedagogical and religious didactic teaching and research, as well as educational work, never occur in a 'vacuum,' but rather always in specific societal, economic, political, cultural, religious and historical contexts.[1] Scientific religious pedagogy and religious didactics necessitate reflection on these contexts. Therefore, we will also undertake to contextualize our interreligious approach. In doing so, we are well aware that these contexts are not 'reality' per se, but rather are based on phenomena that are largely constructed. Hence, we cannot examine every detail of the current contexts, but instead will be content with a general overview and will orient ourselves in accordance with the currently predominant keywords of theory (the general perspective) and life practice (the concrete perspective).

General Perspectives

In this section, we will deal with general contextual aspects, which, in our opinion, shape the current debate on religious education.

Secularity

Christians and Muslims in Europe move – according to general opinion – in a secular space. But this phraseology is not clear, since the word 'secular'

---

1   See Willems, Joachim, *Interreligiöse Kompetenz. Theoretische Grundlagen – Konzeptualisierungen – Unterrichtsmethoden*. Wiesbaden 2011, 65.

has a range of different meanings and connotations. Furthermore, there are different perspectives on the term 'secular.' Thus, at least among Christians and Muslims, some religious people also view themselves as secular. But the opposite is also the case. Some religious people distance themselves from the secular and perceive it as a 'counterpart' that is not compatible with their religious convictions. In fundamentalist circles, this can go so far that it is said that it is necessary to fight against the secular in order to enforce 'religion' in society.

Ingolf Dalferth draws attention to the fact that the word 'secular' is always understood against the backdrop of and as dependent on 'religious.' This is the basis for a dualistic tension, which Dalferth describes as follows:

> In the concept of the secular lies a reference to the religious, which cannot be faded out without emptying the term. This does not apply to the religious. One can live religiously without making reference to the secular: The meaning of the expression 'religious' is not always determined in contrast to 'secular'. However, one cannot live secularly without demarcating oneself from the religious: The meaning of the expression 'secular' always includes a relationship of negation with regard to 'religious'.[2]

Dalferth distinguishes ways of speaking about the 'secular' and considers it meaningful to reconsider the concept of secularism and – in order to overcome the dualism – to speak of 'post-secular' at the level of states and societies.[3] Other authors also demand a more precise differentiation of the concept of secularity and distinguish several meanings for it.[4] In this regard, Charles Taylor argues that secularity can be and has been understood primarily as a 'decline of religion in public life.'[5]

---

2   Dalferth, Ingolf U., Religionsfixierte Moderne? Der lange Weg vom säkularen Zeitalter zur post-säkularen Welt. In: *Denkströme. Journal der Sächsischen Akademie der Wissenschaften* (2011) 7, 9–32, 9.
3   See ibid., 25–31.
4   See Taylor, Charles, *Ein säkulares Zeitalter*. Frankfurt a. M. 2012, 703f; cf. also Palaver, Wolfgang, Christentum im säkularen Kontext. Grenzen und Chancen. In: Kästle, Daniela, Kraml, Martina, and Mohagheghi, Hamideh (eds.), *Heilig-Tabu. Christen und Muslime wagen Begegnungen* (Kommunikative Theologie, Vol. 13). Ostfildern 2009, 311–318, 311f.
5   Taylor, *Ein säkulares Zeitalter*, 332.

Specifically in Europe, this implies that religion, in its traditional form, is a cause of violence, terror and war and should therefore be banned from the public space. Rendering secularity a religion-free public space would guarantee, according to this thesis, freedom and democracy. José Casanova highlights the problematic nature of this perception and points out that violence and anti-democratic actions also occur in secular spaces.[6] In the context of understandings of secularity that propagate a contradiction between religion and the secular world, one could speak of freedom *from* religion. Hans-Joachim Höhn warns against uncritically propagating or overstating not only the thesis of secularization in the sense of the demise of religions, but also the thesis of the return of religions. He calls for differentiation and identifies 'processes for the heterogeneous transformation of the religious,'[7] the description of which requires differentiated theoretical models that can correspond to 'processes of cultural, social and political modernization.'[8]

Another model, outlined by Charles Taylor, understands secularity as a process that allows for freedom of religion in the first place. One could designate this freedom *for* religion. According to Taylor, the new temporal thinking of 'immanent humanism'[9] is decisive. It emphasizes the naturalness of religion and its orientation toward moral principles, such as diligence and purposefulness, as well as the neutrality of desire.[10] This way of thinking, described by Taylor as an 'exclusionary humanism,'[11] which proliferated from the seventeenth and eighteenth centuries onward and became an 'ever more viable spiritual conception,'[12] assumes that man alone can effect – intrinsically – his own destiny and well-being, without recourse to transcendence and ultimately without recourse to God.[13]

6   See Casanova, José, *Europas Angst vor der Religion*. Berlin 2009.
7   Höhn, Hans-Joachim, Reflexive Modernisierung – reflexive Säkularisierung. In: Gmainer-Pranzl, Franz, and Rettenbacher, Sigrid (eds.), *Religion in postsäkularer Gesellschaft. Interdisziplinäre Perspektiven* (Salzburger interdisziplinäre Diskurse, Vol. 3). Frankfurt a. M. 2013, 15–34, 34.
8   See ibid., 34.
9   Taylor, *Ein säkulares Zeitalter*, 441.
10 See ibid., 393–396.
11 Ibid., 401.
12 Ibid.
13 See ibid., 402.

> It is obvious that this more recent humanism, in a certain sense, differentiates itself from most of the ancient ethics of human nature, in that it is marginal, in other words, in that its conception of human prosperity does not refer to anything higher that people should worship, love or acknowledge.[14]

According to Taylor, this thesis brought a new option into play. Henceforth, there were several possibilities for structuring life: that which recognizes or reckons with God and those that do not need God for their conception of life and the world, as well as personal prosperity. The 'secular age,' in Taylor's understanding, is thus characterized by options, of which faith is only one. Accordingly, one could also refer to this period as the age of decisions or freedom of choice.

Wolfgang Palaver takes this as his point of departure. He also links secularity to agency and opines that the experience of secularity in this sense leads us to expect freedom:[15]

> This third form of secularity is particularly important for our reflection on our situation as Christians in our present world. Today, we are experiencing a world of ever-expanding freedom. [...] The experience that we could do things differently has become a fundamental characteristic of our world.[16]

What Palaver speaks of here, we will refer to later as 'contingency awareness' or 'possibility awareness.' He quotes Dostoyevsky's *The Brothers Karamazov* to describe the 'burden of freedom':[17]

> Instead of taking over the freedom of the people, you have made it even greater! Have you forgotten that peace and even death are dearer to men than freedom of choice in the knowledge of good and evil? Nothing is as seductive to man as the freedom of his conscience, but there is nothing that torments him more. And now, instead of the fixed principles of a conscience that has been steadily settled, you have chosen everything that is exceptional, puzzling and vacillating, everything that goes beyond the powers of man. You act as if you do not love them – of all people, you![18]

---

14 Ibid., 420.
15 See Palaver, Christentum im säkularen Kontext, 312.
16 Ibid., 312f.
17 Ibid., 313.
18 Dostoyevsky, Fyodor, *The Brothers Karamazov*. Cited in: Palaver, Christentum im säkularen Kontext, 313.

When we speak about the concept of secularism in the context of a Muslim–Christian project, it should be noted that Christianity and Islam have been historically shaped by different societal and political developments. The legacy of the Enlightenment tradition, as it manifests itself in Europe, is characterized by an understanding of emancipation from denominational authoritarian church structures. The bond of religion was contrasted with the autonomous, responsible and self-determined person. As for the Muslim context, it is true that, due to other societal factors, authoritarian religious structures were not dealt with in the same way they were dealt with in Europe. This does not mean that in the Muslim context attempts have not been made – and are not being made – to emerge from 'self-inflicted immaturity.'[19] In relation to this, Heiner Bielefeld warns against a 'culturalist monopolization of secularity.'[20] In this context, a culturalist monopolization of secularity would mean the exclusive application of the secular rule of law in the part of Europe that has been shaped by Christianity.[21] Bielefeld writes:

> For the sake of the equal freedom and equal right of participation for all in the multicultural and multireligious society, the rule of law must refrain from propagating the dominant constitutional principles, in the manner presented by Huntington, as the exclusive heritage of Western Christian civilization. The fact that the secular rule of law became historically effective for the first time in North America and Western Europe remains undisputed. However, restricting the validity of the secular constitutional model to Western civilization and culture would be politically treacherous and a legally rash act.[22]

That the secular rule of law has not been established in many so-called Muslim countries may also be due to the circumstances of their first encounters with secular society, which in some regions proceeded in a very

---

19   See Ebert, Hans-Georg (ed.), *Der Islam und die Grundlagen der Herrschaft. Übersetzung und Kommentar des Werkes von Alî Abd ar-Râziq*. Frankfurt a. M. 2010.
20   See Bielefeldt, Heiner, *Muslime im säkularen Rechtsstaat. Integrationschancen durch Religionsfreiheit*. Bielefeld 2003, 48–58.
21   See Bielefeldt, Heiner, Muslimische Minderheiten im säkularen Rechtsstaat. In: Bukow, Wolf-Dietrich, and Yildiz, Erol (eds.), *Islam und Bildung* (Interkulturelle Studien, Vol. 15). Opladen 2003, 21–36.
22   Ibid., 28f.

unfortunate manner as a result of colonization. The encounter between Muslims and the secular rule of law, represented by the colonial powers, which often acted in ways that were not in keeping with the secular rule of law in the colonized territories, inevitably created an aversion to everything that the colonial powers represented. All too often, the encounter with colonial powers was associated with defeat, surrender and humiliation, which further increased resistance to and skepticism toward secularism. This trauma, which was compounded by other factors, such as the abuse of secularity as a substitute religion by some Muslim dictators, persists among many Muslims to this day.[23] These brief explanations illustrate that the concept of secularity is very complex for religious people, especially for Muslims and Christians.

In the course of the migration movements that took place from the 1960s onwards, this complexity was hardly noticed at first. Only through increased visibility, and greater participation of Muslims in society did the historical differences become clearer. In addition, the experiences of Muslims and non-Muslims are divergent: The fact that Muslims live their religion publicly and take it seriously surprised many non-Muslim Europeans. As a result, the following questions, among others, have emerged: Why do so many Muslims practice their religion so consistently? Why do they stick to the prohibitions and laws of their religion so strictly? Why are clothing and food rules religiously justified? Why is there no critical approach to religion? Why is there no separation of religion and state in the minds of many Muslims?

Moreover, people in Europe have experienced and continue to experience the withdrawal of religion into the private sphere (privatization). Islam, however, is seen as a religion that has not undergone privatization, thereby breaking with European tradition. On the basis of its history, European tradition harbors the suspicion that religions – above all monotheistic ones – prevent diversity through their claim to truth and thus promote

---

23 See Sejdini, Zekirija, Zwischen Gewissheit und Kontingenz. Auf dem Weg zu einem neuen Verständnis von islamischer Theologie und Religionspädagogik im europäischen Kontext. In: Sejdini, Zekirija (ed.), *Islamische Theologie und Religionspädagogik in Bewegung. Neue Ansätze in Europa*. Bielefeld 2016, 15–31, here 26.

intolerance and even violence.[24] The implicitly or explicitly accompanying thesis reads as follows: As long as religion is 'tamed' and 'cherished and provided for' in the private sphere, it appears harmless to Western society, because control and damage limitation are possible. When religion becomes publicly visible, as in the case of Islam, it becomes suspicious and dangerous. The current efforts to implement the *burka* and *burkini* ban demonstrate the increased interest in the establishment of control mechanisms. Another example is *racial profiling*, whereby stereotypes and external features lead, for example, to Muslims in public spaces being monitored more often than non-Muslims.[25] Furthermore, the appearance of Islam, with its symbolic forms of expression, in the European context recalls the repressed 'old struggles' of Western societies with authoritarian denominational forms of religion and sets in motion corresponding mechanisms.

Denominationality

In the context of religious education in schools in Austria and in most German federal states, the term 'denominationality,' which was originally linked to Christian churches, has been extended to other religious communities in discussions of 'denominational religious instruction.' Strictly speaking, in the legal sense, the correct phraseology should be 'denominational religious instruction and religious instruction for which religious communities are responsible.' This responsibility refers to the rights of the churches and religious communities, which – in Austria and Germany – are regulated differently in relation to the development of

24   See Assmann, Jan, *Monotheismus und die Sprache der Gewalt*. Vienna 2009.
25   On the meaning of *racial profiling*: 'The term comes from the USA, where mainly African Americans and people of Latin American descent are affected by an above-average number of police identity checks. It is also spoken by ethnic profiling. In the European context, not only black people but also persons from the Balkan region (especially the Roma) as well as from Arab countries and Muslims are affected by unjustified personal and vehicle controls' (Verein humanrights.ch (ed.), Rassistisches Profiling: Begriff und Problematik. Internet resource: <http://www.humanrights.ch/de/menschenrechte-themen/rassismus/rassistisches-profiling/begriff/> [accessed on February 18, 2017]).

curricula and school supervision. The inaccurate usage of the word 'denomination,' in addition to the legal aspects, indicates deeper misunderstandings and questions associated with the term 'denominationality.' In the European context, 'denominational' is generally understood 'as a commitment to a particular institutionalized form of religious doctrine and practice.'[26]

The secularization thesis involves a range of misunderstandings. It turns out that the suspicion that religion will incite violence and the secularist need for 'damage limitation' through the privatization of religion in Europe are not primarily related to Islam. From a historical point of view, questions relating to the confrontation with or limitation of religion in the public domain originally arose from the question of denomination within Christianity. These questions derived from the differing opinions regarding the claim to truth within Christianity and the necessity of safeguarding the terrain between the Christian churches. In the so-called wars of religion, which originally focused on the question of the 'right religion' within Christianity, that is, the 'right denomination,' the 'truth' – mixed with societal and political interests – was also fought for using violence. According to J. Casanova, 'Europe's fear of religion'[27] did not originally refer to Islam, as it now does, at least partially, in late modern Europe, but rather to other denominations, with their violently asserted truth claims, or to Christianity as a whole.

Furthermore, it should be borne in mind that the Enlightenment ideal was 'natural religiosity' – in the sense of a 'natural attachment' of man – and thus a conflict existed between 'natural religiosity' and denominational religion. The positive connotations of natural religiosity and its propagation to the detriment of denominational manifestations of religion have also shaped the history of Christian religious pedagogy. On the one hand, the distinction was made between a general – non-denominationally connoted – religious education and the transmission of sets of beliefs

26 Ziebertz, Hans-Georg, Der Beitrag der christlichen Theologie zur Imameausbildung. In: Ucar, Bülent (ed.), *Imamausbildung in Deutschland. Islamische Theologie im europäischen Kontext* (Veröffentlichungen des Zentrums für Interkulturelle Islamstudien der Universität Osnabrück, Vol. 3). Göttingen 2010, 289–305, 291.
27 See Casanova, *Europas Angst vor der Religion*.

(catechesis) anchored in the catechisms, and, on the other hand, religious pedagogy was established as the more open, wider and more scientific alternative to the catechetics, whose ecclesiastical contamination is viewed with skepticism.

As with many terms that originally arose in the Christian European context, the transference of the term 'denominationality' to Islam has been attended by many difficulties.[28] The fact that, by virtue of the legal situation and denominationally anchored religious education, Muslim representations in Europe have long since discovered the significance of denominationality should not obscure these difficulties.

But since Islam does not have a church structure, the use of the term 'denomination-oriented'[29] seems to be more appropriate in this context. However, this is not intended to hide the fact that Muslims are also divided into different groups that consider themselves to be separate them from one another, theologically and politically. It is only intended to draw attention to a phenomenon that is too often evident in interreligious encounters when using concepts that have emerged in different contexts. Not infrequently, different interpretations of certain terms lead to failure in interreligious conversations.

In sum, denominationality has long been understood in Europe as an internal differentiation of Christianity. The concept is associated with the 'stable odor' of the clergy. In the context of Catholicism and Protestantism, it was often used to counteract developments of interreligiosity. From this analysis of the situation it becomes clear that without ignoring the significance and burden of the historical conflicts among the Christian churches and the Islamic traditions, we must redefine the concept of denominationality in the context of interreligiosity. In the fourth chapter, we will therefore pursue a possible new understanding of denominationality, one that is not fixated on separation, but rather has at its heart the gift of diversity.

---

28   See Renz, Andreas, *Der Mensch unter dem An-Spruch Gottes. Offenbarungsverständnis und Menschenbild des Islam im Urteil gegenwärtiger christlicher Theologie* (Christentum und Islam, Vol. 1). Würzburg 2002, 23.
29   Ziebertz, Der Beitrag der christlichen Theologie zur Imameausbildung, 291.

Plurality: Heterogeneity

If one searches for the term 'plurality' on the Google Books Ngram Viewer,[30] one will see that the term has only been used widely since the mid-twentieth century.

In the Christian European context, despite denominational differences, religious plurality was scarcely perceived as a plurality because the focus was more on one's own denomination, in the sense of an *in-group*. Thus, a strong internal–external contradistinction was constructed. Once the outside came into view, it was immediately evaluated in relation to one's own denomination and then either included or excluded. It was the different ecumenical movements – for which the Catholic side, above all in the Ecumenism Decree of the Second Vatican Council,[31] provided the language – that raised awareness of the plurality of Christian denominations and the opportunity for 'unity in diversity.' Until then, plurality had been understood more as a disruption than an enrichment. Likewise, in the Islamic tradition, awareness is primarily focused on one's own group. However, in some phases of history, according to authors such as Thomas Bauer, a higher level of tolerance for ambiguity, in terms of diversity, is attributed to this tradition, particularly regarding the variety of readings of the Qur'an.[32] The absence of an institutionalized authority, such as that of the Christian churches, further favored the recognition of diversity. This may be surprising in the present context since a different image prevails in the media, as well as in educational contexts, in which Islam is associated with violence. This violence is often linked to the verbal inspiration of the Arabic Qur'an. The perception has been widely circulated that the Qur'an may not be translated or interpreted, which does not reflect the historical evolution of Islam or the contemporary reality.

For a wide variety of reasons (such as, for example, occupational mobility, the new media, globalization and migration movements), plurality,

---

30 For this purpose Google Books Ngram Viewer (<https://books.google.com/ngrams> [accessed on February 23, 2017]) German Literature from 1600 to 2008 was retrieved.
31 See Second Vatican Council, Decree on *oecumenicae navitatis unitatis redintegratio*.
32 See Bauer, Thomas, *Die Kultur der Ambiguität. Eine andere Geschichte des Islams*. Berlin 2011, 56.

including religious ideological plurality, has become a reality. It pervades society and triggers a wide range of reactions: Some consider diversity a threat and denounce positive attitudes toward diversity as relativism, while others view diversity exclusively as an enrichment and an opportunity, thus ignoring both the challenges and limitations.

Likewise, it can be observed that the 'other side' is considered to be more homogeneous than is actually the case. Thus, a monolithic Islam is frequently talked about, without taking into consideration the many traditions and cultures denoted by 'Islam.' Paul Mecheril points out that, in the 'discursive constructions' of Western actors, Islam is 'constructed as a homogenous group, which differs fundamentally from the way its own group perceives it. [...] Islam becomes the other, the unfamiliar religion. This occurs within and through diverse practices (medial, societal political, academic, etc.) of exclusion, attribution, hierarchization, differentiation, homogenization and essentialization.'[33]

A central challenge for an interreligious religious pedagogy and religious didactics, which relates to the design of educational processes, consists of cultivating and living according to an appropriate way of dealing with the most varied forms of religious and (socio-)cultural plurality.

Concrete Perspectives

At this point, we take a closer look at concrete aspects that determine current educational contexts and especially the Christianity–Islam–secular world relationship.

In general, one can say that this relationship has always been defined very schematically. This is still the case today, even if new categorizations (e.g. equating Islamic traditions or Muslims with violent and terrorist movements) have replaced the old ones. On the one hand, in this book, we address such categorizations, as they are part of the context in which

33 Lingen-Ali, Ulrike, and Mecheril, Paul, Religion als soziale Deutungspraxis. In: *Österreichisches Religionspädagogisches Forum* (2016) 2, 17–24, 19.

we live. On the other hand, we want to demonstrate that a hermeneutics that portrays Islam as a homogenous field and, furthermore, as fixated on violence, terror or immigration, represents a constriction that often goes hand in hand with castigation.

Violence, Terror and Right-Wing Populism

Since September 11, 2001, discussions about the connection between violence and religion have been in the consciousness of a broad public. Religiously connoted violent and terrorist movements are frightening many people and engendering powerlessness and helplessness. Many doubt the humanizing potential of religion. The fascination with radical movements, which also affects young people in fundamentally democratic societies, represents a major educational challenge.

The current public consciousness primarily and almost exclusively links movements that promote violence and terror to Islam. Thus, in Western media, positive aspects of Islam, such as Arabic calligraphy, art, poetry, hospitality, etc., are no longer being thematized. Instead, the focus is exclusively on negative constructs. By allowing the discourse to be determined by extreme groups, Western societies and the media are contributing to the radicalization of Islamic groups. An important phenomenon, which is usually ignored in this context, but which plays a major role, is the growing right-wing populism in European countries. Although right-wing populism is a well-known phenomenon in European history, at present Muslim-motivated terrorist violence and refugee movements affecting large numbers of Muslims are being used by various political forces to incite xenophobia and thereby strengthen their own positions.

Refugee Movements

The large refugee movements of 2015 and 2016 and the unpredictability of the future massively challenge those who work in educational institutions and those who are in charge in educational institutions. The resulting transformation and reshuffling processes have affected the religious sphere in particular. Contrary to the public perception, the refugees belong to very different religious denominations. While the majority of the refugees are Muslims from different traditions, a significant number are Christians. As a consequence of the refugee movements, religious and cultural pluralization has accelerated enormously. There is a dearth of ideas and solutions aimed at acknowledging this plurality and handling the accompanying phenomena in an appropriate and interculturally and interreligiously sensitive manner.

Initially, the refugee movements, particularly in German-speaking countries, triggered the broad engagement of the civilian population. Over time, and due to reactions from the populist political parties, the public commitment gave way to skepticism: Fears arose regarding the social system and discouragement and overstraining became apparent. The radicalization of young people, provoked by certain Islamic groups, on the one hand, and the exploitation of people for the dubious political aims of far-right parties, on the other, became evident. Moreover, it turns out that adequate resources for the individual psychological, social societal, cultural and religious integration of the refugees were lacking. Many had had traumatic experiences in their countries of origin or while fleeing. The possibilities for obtaining professional help and processing those experiences are very limited.

Immigration Society

We are aware that immigration is multifaceted and affects people from different cultures and religions. As this book is concerned with Christianity and Islam, we concentrate on these perspectives and on Muslim immigration.

Since the 1960s, Muslims who came as part of labor migrations have been living in Austria, Germany and other European countries in large numbers. Of course, historically, Muslims lived in territories belonging to the Austro-Hungarian monarchy. Because of their allegiance to the state, they were legally and practically equated with Protestants. Austria's Islam Law, which, among other things, provides the right to Islamic religious education in schools, goes back to the days of the monarchy. Muslims practice their religion and culture in everyday life, with the result that this has essentially become an integral part of everyday culture and thus also of the majority society. But Islam is not well anchored in the consciousness of the majority society, which means that this reality is not seen and taken seriously.[34]

Furthermore, an unequal or asymmetrical hermeneutics and perspective on the part of the majority society is evidenced by the fact that Muslims are viewed as a separate prominent group that has become the object of 'measures' or 'treatment,' such as, for example, the ban on religious symbols that applies exclusively to Muslims.[35] Often Muslims are not permitted to occupy some public spaces as a matter of course and are only able to observe and live in accordance with their requirements as Muslims to a limited extent. Moreover, their religion is not considered simply a religion among other 'self-evident' religions or denominations, but rather is highlighted as deficient or violent. Consequently, Muslims experience a kind of isolation, life in the 'underground' and 'exoticization.'[36] According to Bukow, Islam in Western society is strongly linked to the question of immigration:

> Once the discourse on Islam merges with the immigration discourse, it also shares its fate, namely that the Federal Republic still denies that it is an immigration country, and as a result, it also refuses to acknowledge and constructively deal with immigration and all its related aspects. This denial of a largely successful immigration tacitly implants itself in *a denial of Islam as a religion alive here today and locally in everyday life*, as a religious orientation rooted in urban coexistence.[37]

---

34   See Bukow, Wolf-Dietrich, Der Islam – ein bildungspolitisches Thema. In: Bukow, Wolf-Dietrich, and Yildiz, Erol (eds.), *Islam und Bildung* (Interkulturelle Studien, Vol. 15). Opladen 2003, 57–80.

35   See in this regard the findings on *racial profiling*: Verein humanrights.ch (ed.), Rassistisches Profiling; see also the discussion of the ban on religious symbols, such the headscarf, as a female or male judge, at the police station, etc.; see the Austrian debate about the draft of the law to ban the *burka* in the spring of 2017: Mittelstaedt, Katharina, Regierung einigt sich auf Burkaverbot im 'neutral auftretenden' Staat. Internet resource: <http://derstandard.at/2000051810497/Regierung-einigt-sich-auf-Burkaverbot-im-neutral-auftretenden-Staat> [accessed on February 23, 2017].

36   Bukow, Der Islam – ein bildungspolitisches Thema, 65f.

37   Ibid., 65.

A serious consideration of these aspects and facets of the phenomena of violence and terror, and refugee movements and the problems of the society receiving migrants, reveals major challenges for the entire educational system with regard to the different worlds that encounter one another, the importance of religion and relationships of interaction and communication. Specifically, all of this affects an interreligiously oriented religious pedagogy and religious didactics.

Challenges for the Educational Context

Educational institutions, specifically the schools, are not well prepared for plurality contexts. In Austria, the country's status as an immigration society has not yet been accepted as self-evident. In addition, the educational institutions are for the most part overwhelmed, in particular in the context of refugee movements. Refugees' traumatizing experiences of terror and violence can rarely be dealt with adequately. The necessary human resources, financial and professional personnel are, for the most part, not available. Professionals specialized in immigration and refugee situations and appropriate training in these areas in are urgently needed, but hardly in sight.

People's religious needs also present specific challenges. The privatization of religion, which is indirectly or directly propagated in the European context, presents a problem. For example, most refugees and migrants are used to a way of dealing with religion that is different from what they find in most European, including German-speaking, countries. Muslims, in particular, are torn between different 'worlds.' Moreover, as has already been mentioned several times, they are confronted with the fact that Islam is not regarded as a self-evident religion in the European context. Thus, many young Muslims, for example, try to reconcile the different values and worlds. Nikola Tietze writes:

> Young Muslims are individuals who have fully embraced modernity. They integrate Islam into the contradictions, as well as the increasing acceleration of social changes.

In this way, they can develop an autonomy that precludes a simple submission to the rules of religious dogma and a dissolution of individuality in the community.[38]

Often the attempt to mediate these values is made overly challenging by the actions of the majority society.

The language constructed by the majority society, involving differentiations and categorizations, plays an important role in the emergence and transmission of asymmetrical hermeneutics and perspectives (Muslims as 'objects'; one-sided viewpoints, such as those that focus on Muslims and not vice versa; the perception of the Muslim perspective, etc.). To raise awareness of this and to oppose it with a new perspective, or a new 'framing,'[39] is the task of a religion- and plurality-sensitive education and therefore also a religion- and plurality-sensitive pedagogy and didactics.

Consequences for an Interreligious Religious Pedagogy and Religious Didactics

In view of the above spotlight-style description of the Western and Central European context, and of our concerns, it becomes clear that the current situation is of decisive significance for religious pedagogical and religious didactic action. Due to the fact that the context we live in is characterized by constant change, empirical analyses of individual perspectives or societal tendencies are imperative for religious pedagogy and religious didactics. Furthermore, language, symbolization, differentiation and categorization play an essential role in the construction of social relationships. Therefore, it is the task of education and therefore the task of

---

38   Tietze, Nikola, Muslimische Identitäten. In: Bukow, Wolf-Dietrich, and Yildiz, Erol (eds.), *Islam und Bildung* (Interkulturelle Studien, Vol. 15). Opladen 2003, 83–91, 90.
39   On the topic of 'framing,' specifically political framing, see: Lakoff, George and Wehling, Elisabeth, *Auf leisen Sohlen ins Gehirn. Politische Sprache und ihre heimliche Macht*. Heidelberg 2008.

critical religious pedagogy and religious didactics to reflect these forms of communication. In the process, it is essential to adjust one's views, while remaining aware, in particular, of one's own blind spots. The result for religious pedagogical and religious didactic teaching and research is that they cannot be satisfied exclusively with analysis, but must also bring forth critical theological interpretations and theoretical explanations.

CHAPTER 2

Anthropology-Theology-Education: Our Agreed-upon Foundations

After having analyzed the context, and against the backdrop of that analysis, we want to reflect on the anthropological, theological and educational theoretical foundations that shape our approach and concepts. Our consideration of the context heightened our sensitivity to the fact that inequalities and imbalances permeate us, and our contexts, and that this can also happen in religious communities and religious education.[1] Thus, we are challenged to critically scrutinize our language, our categorizations and our differentiations for their integrating or excluding impacts.

For this reason, in the first section ('How Do We Understand Being Human?'), we begin with an anthropological trait that characterizes and unites all of us – whether we are Christian or Muslim, people without a denomination or atheists: 'simply being human.' At the same time, we are, as human beings, defined by values and worldviews and, in this respect, aligned with the transcendent. In other words, we are, in this sense, 'religious' people, and our anthropology (our image of humankind) and theology (our understanding of God) shape our values and our worldviews. We will illustrate this interconnection in the second section ('How Do We Understand "God and the World"?'). Finally, in the third section ('Theology as Science from a Religious Pedagogical Perspective'), we will discuss the understanding of education.

How Do We Understand Being Human?

There are many different approaches to the humanity of humans. As pedagogues and didacts of religion, we take a religious pedagogical theological perspective. This raises the question of which concerns should be

---

[1] See Lingen-Ali and Mecheril, Religion als soziale Deutungspraxis, 17.

pursued in the context of a theological anthropology. The central question for a theological understanding of humankind is how human beings can be understood against the background of the question of God. The question of humankind and God, as well as human dignity and reverence for God, are closely related to each other and constitute important life- and action-oriented concepts. It must be added that the question of God from an anthropological perspective can have very different points of departure: man's longing; his ability to ask questions; the witnessing or experiencing of suffering, among others.

When one begins with people's experiences, one finds that images of man and images of being human are very different. This is evident from the fact that in a group of people who want to exchange views about their own images of man, there are difficulties in articulation and different conceptions of being human. When human images are reflected upon, positively connoted images of being human are mentioned in an initial phase of reflection. It is only in the course of a deeper process that the difficulties of anthropological reflection, as well as the ambivalent and fragmentary nature of human existence, come to the fore. Thus, it becomes clear that anthropological images are shaped by their religious ideological, historical and cultural contingency, and therefore are 'never to be determined absolutely'[2] or put too generally. Tied to religious ideological conditionality, the development of anthropological foundations in the framework of our interreligious religious didactics is always shaped by one's perspective. At the same time, in a theological anthropology, the fundamental conceptions of man always refer back to God. This is not contradicted by the fact that people, out of their autonomy and communal relatedness, arrive at conceptions of man that were not and are not directly derived from religious traditions. Human rights, which are recognized in many societies of the world by virtue of their consensual grounding, represent one such secular conception. They affect both religious and non-religious people in the same way. Based on the 'modern achievements' of human rights, this book endeavors to

2   Wulf, Christoph, and Zirfass, Jörg, Homo educandus. Eine Einleitung in die Pädagogische Anthropologie. In: Wulf, Christoph, and Zirfass, Jörg (eds.), *Handbuch pädagogischer Anthropologie*. Wiesbaden 2014, 9–26, 12.

explicate the anthropological foundations that can be reconciled with both human rights and the religious theological understanding of Muslim and Christian traditions. By this we mean that human rights should not be thought of as in contradiction with the religious traditions, but rather should seek to be recognized by the traditions and should also be the basis for any interreligious cooperation.

From the human rights point of view, as well as from the Islamic and Catholic theological-anthropological points of view, three basic perspectives seem to us to be characteristic of being human: relatedness, freedom, and responsibility. They also mark the basic conflicts. These basic perspectives will be elaborated in the next sections in relation to the following aspects: createdness, human dignity, freedom, reason and responsibility. In the last part of the anthropological section, we will deal with being human under concrete contextual conditions.

Createdness

A basic anthropological experience shared by Christians and Muslims is the createdness of humankind and the world. In contrast to a naturalistic understanding of humankind and the world, religious people are guided by the insight that they are not living on their own, but instead are based in a reality that infinitely transcends humans and the world. In different religions, the existence of man is associated with the recognition of a divine reality in various ways. Transcendent reality is related to humankind and at the same time we are deprived of access to it and it remains the ultimate secret of life.

From this point of view, humankind is neither at the mercy of appropriation by worldly things, which a technocratic economic worldview tends toward, nor are we disconnected and separated from the world – as if the future of the world and humankind would leave us untouched. The creation-related view gives rise to a new perspective, with the result that the human being, who thinks and feels in a creation-related manner, can recognize and comprehend the gift of the universal reality of life, and live gratefully for having been given it.

This is also the concern of the Qur'anic and Biblical texts. They tell of the creation of humankind and the world through the one and only God based on a free divine decision.[3] Regardless of how differently these textual sources on God's creation within and between these religions have been and will continue to be interpreted, the recognition of a good creation of humankind and the world constitutes a fundamental connection between these religions.

The biblical texts tell of the free and good creation of God. A literal approach to the texts on creation to explain scientific phenomena has been cultivated for centuries and has led to many misunderstandings and inequitable judgments in dealing with modern natural sciences into modern times, but this seems to have been overcome. Thus, an evolutionary and a Christian or Muslim view of man and the world are no longer necessarily in contradiction with one another. The core of the biblical understanding of man, which is metaphorically expressed in the texts on creation, is the image of the breath of God (*ruach*) in man. God breathes into the 'earthling,' making him a living man (see Gen. 2:7). The relatedness of man cannot be expressed more primordially: God breathes and lives in him. In the mystical life cultures of different, mostly Eastern religions, being present in the breath has a special significance and establishes a deep connection to the so-called revelatory religions' understanding of human nature.

A fundamental misunderstanding in Christian interpretation lies in the conception of the mastery of creation, as if creation were the property of humankind and subject to his arbitrariness. The belief that ultimately everything belongs to God guides people to their role in the joint concern for the good life and the maintenance of creation.

Man's createdness is also of central importance in Islamic anthropology. In a world in which everything (except God) is contingent – that is, possible and not necessary and thus differing fundamentally from God, as a necessary being – the connection with the Creator, from an Islamic perspective, represents an important anthropological foundation. From the Qur'anic perspective, man was created from different elements and had

---

[3] See Qur'an, 2:30–35; see, among others, both Biblical creation texts Gen. 1:1–2,4 and Gen. 2:4–25 and the so-called creation psalm 104.

to go through several stages of development[4] before being made human by the breath of the Divine Spirit.[5] Thus, he transformed from a pure wet clay mass, or from a physical being, into a spiritual being, in other words, into a 'new man,' endowed with the Divine Spirit and mental, as well as spiritual, capabilities, to which nothing need be added.[6] The breathing in of the Divine Spirit filled the mere form with life and gave it the potential to serve as an intercessor (*khalifa*)[7] of God. This is also the basis of the special position of man within the entire creation. Yet, this special position of man is, as was mentioned earlier in the Christian context, not only a privilege, but also brings with it a great responsibility for all of creation, which is entrusted to him for his use. The concept of the entrustment (*amana*) of all of creation to man should make it clear that this is in no way a perpetual possession, but only a time-limited disposition, for which responsibility must be assumed before God.[8]

Seen in this way, man in his createdness is also completely dependent on God from the Islamic anthropological perspective.

Human Dignity

From a theological anthropological perspective, createdness is based on the relationship between the creature and the Creator. For religious people, it forms the foundation of human dignity. Human dignity in turn is closely related to human rights. Human rights can be understood as a modern exploration of human dignity and an endeavor to give this dignity, which belongs to every human being, a legally binding and

4   See Qur'an: 15:26; 32:7; 76:1–2; 96:2.
5   See Qur'an: 38:72; 32:9; 15:29.
6   See Hajatpour, Reza, Mensch und Gott. Von islamisch-philosophischen Menschenbildern. In: Behr, Harry Harun, and Ulfat, Fahimah (eds.), *Zwischen Himmel und Erde. Bildungsphilosophische Verhältnisbestimmungen von Heiligem Text und Geist*. Münster 2014, 77–90, 79.
7   See Qur'an: 2:30.
8   See Sejdini, Zekirija, Armutsbekämpfung und Gerechtigkeit aus islamischer Perspektive. In: Ströbele, Christian et al. (eds.), *Armut und Gerechtigkeit. Christliche und islamische Perspektiven*. Regensburg 2016, 295–300, 297f.

sanctionable basis. The starting point of human rights is the inviolable dignity of man. From a Muslim, as well as a Christian, perspective, human dignity, as an anthropological foundation, is beyond question.[9] In the Christian and Muslim sources, for example, there are numerous passages in which reference is made to the dignity of humankind – and there are also references to the equal dignity of men and women. Some of these specifically address the issue of dignity, while others can be interpreted as doing so. The central Qur'anic passage that directly refers to the divine dignity of all people is in Sura 17:70. It states:

> NOW, INDEED, We have conferred dignity on the children of Adam, and borne them over land and sea, and provided for them sustenance out of the good things of life, and favoured them far above most of Our creation.[10]

In addition to this central point, there are many other references in the Qur'an that highlight the dignity of humankind, including, among others, the creation of man in the best possible form (32:7), the breathing in of the Divine Spirit (32:9), as well as man's designation as God's intercessor on earth (2:30).

The Bible also contains a rich body of statements on human dignity. Gen. 1:27 states that man is God's image. This picture demonstrates the inalienable dignity of humankind. In Psalm 8, humankind is endowed, by God, with 'glory and honor': 'You have made him only a little less than God' (Ps. 8:6). In the New Testament and in the Christian tradition, human dignity is exemplified in the demeanor of Jesus when he encounters and identifies with the people, especially the disadvantaged and the persecuted. It is he who restores the people's dignity, which had been trampled on (Luke 7:36–50, 19:1–10, John 8:1–11 and others). The double commandment of love (Matt. 22:36–40) also expresses the value of a human being. This concerns the dignity of both women and men. In Christianity, the position of women, especially in the New Testament, was repeatedly brought up. Jesus himself criticized the marginalization

---

9   See Bielefeldt, Heiner, *Menschenrechte in der Einwanderungsgesellschaft. Plädoyer für einen aufgeklärten Multikulturalismus*. Bielefeld 2015, 41.
10 Asad, Muhammad, *The Message of the Qur'an*. Bristol 2003, 478.

of women in society at that time. He had female disciples in his company, women were the first witnesses of the resurrection and social patterns of discrimination against women were made visible, such as, for example, the pericope with the adulteress (John 8:1–11) or the divorce laws (Luke 16:16–18).

At the time of the founding of Islam, there was a special sensitivity to the position of the woman, even against the background of the prevailing customs and traditions: The woman was assigned no original sin, received the right of inheritance and was no longer regarded simply as a possession. However, over the course of the development of Islamic theology and society, little account has been taken of this. The foundations laid in the early days have not been further developed. The understanding that one can only remain faithful to the tradition if one constantly renews oneself was lacking. The religious provisions concerning women's rights are not a definitive norm that cannot be improved, but a basic foundation of rights that must not be undercut.

In sum, respect for the dignity of man and the recognition of human rights go hand in hand. They are a fundamental prerequisite for the equal rights of all people and thus they form the basis of any education, particularly interreligious education.

Freedom as an Expression of Createdness and Human Dignity

Human dignity is closely linked to freedom. The limits of freedom are, however, a controversial point among theologians. Not infrequently, the basic relatedness of humankind to God, fellow human beings and the world is considered to be in contradiction with our individual freedom. This is the case, for example, when only the autonomy of the (modern) person is emphasized and his/her fundamental relatedness is forgotten.

Human freedom is one of the most controversial topics in Islamic theological and philosophical history. From the earliest beginnings of the religion to the present, Muslim theologians and philosophers have grappled with the nature and limitations of human freedom. In the process, various currents have emerged that represented, and continue to represent, contradictory positions.[11]

This is because, on the one hand, the various Islamic schools of thought have adopted different epistemological approaches and, on the other hand, the primary Islamic source, the Qur'an, contains ambivalent statements that allow divergent interpretations. Thus, in the Qur'an there are verses that recognize human freedom and highlight the personal responsibility of humankind,[12] as well as verses that give the impression that man has no free will and only lives out his predestined fate.[13] In view of these ambivalent statements, a deeper analysis of the topic seems to be of particular importance, because a narrow conception of man's predestination, which is not infrequently represented, would contradict both the principle of human dignity and the idea of man's personal responsibility, which are also enshrined in the Qur'an.

A closer analysis of the Qur'an leaves no doubt that the overall characteristic style and approach of the Qur'an supports the idea of human free will. For this, a special hermeneutic approach to the Qur'an, which allows for a distinction between 'predestinarian language' and 'predestinarian doctrine,' is required,[14] since, in contrast to the predestinarian language that is used in various Qur'an passages, it is not possible to derive a predestinarian doctrine from the Qur'an. Unlike the doctrine, the language merely aims to emphasize God's omnipotence and make it clear that humankind, which does not have unlimited free will, has obtained freedom not against the will of God, but through the explicit desire and permission of God. Thus, one could say that humankind is predestined to have its own will and that free will is an essential feature of humankind. Lahbabi clearly expresses

---

11   See Wielandt, Rotraud, Der Mensch und seine Stellung in der Schöpfung. Zum Grundverständnis islamischer Anthropologie. In: Bsteh, Andreas, and Hagemann, Ludwig (eds.), *Der Islam als Anfrage an christliche Theologie und Philosophie. Referate – Anfragen – Diskussionen* (Christentum in der Begegnung). Mödling 1994, 97–105, 101–103.
12   See Qur'an: 6:164.
13   See Qur'an: 9:51; 57:22.
14   Renz attributes this very applicable distinction to Räisänen and van Ess; see Renz, *Der Mensch unter dem An-Spruch Gottes*, 382.

this in his book on Islamic anthropology when he writes: 'Autonomy is not a notion of the mind, but rather a fundamental, natural basic structure of our being.'[15]

Likewise, in Christian theology, the subject of human freedom and God's action has been discussed over the centuries. From a historical theological perspective, the question of the relationship between human works and divine grace in the context of Christian doctrines of justification, and the question of the freedom of humankind in the face of divine omnipotence can be mentioned as examples.

From the biblical point of view, the createdness and dignity of humankind are inalienably bound to our freedom, a freedom that even allows us to act contrary to the Creator and to spoil the originally good creation. Dramatically, the Bible tells of the abuse of freedom on the part of humankind: Man wants to be like God (see Gen. 3), kills his brother (Gen. 4:1–16) and tends toward evil (see Gen. 6). Although God 'regretted' that He created man and experiences hurt in His 'heart' as a result of how man abuses his God-given freedom, the Great Flood (Gen. 6–8) is not the last word of God. Rather, God makes a 'covenant' with man in the person of Noah, along with his family, the last survivors, and with all living things, promising that never again will a 'flood' eradicate all of humanity. In the New Testament, the tension between sin and grace mentioned in relation to Paul could be cited here (see Rom. 5). The New Testament, with its conception of the 'new' covenant of God in Jesus, connects to creation and the 'old' covenant of God with man.

One must keep in mind that, in order to successfully be human in freedom, it is essential to consider the contexts of freedom. Our traditions give us important hints in relation to this. First, God gave us our concern for the inviolable dignity of humankind. Dignity implies a recognition of the freedom of every human being. It is a good that people cannot give themselves, but that has been given to them and thus is not subject to their power. On the basis of human dignity, we understand human beings not as individuals, but rather as beings characterized by relatedness. Thus, the

---

15 Lahbabi, Mohammed Aziz, *Der Mensch: Zeuge Gottes. Entwurf einer islamischen Anthropologie*. Freiburg i. Br. 2011, 91.

freedom of one affects the freedom of others. In the sense of human dignity and mutual recognition, it cannot be a question of the limitless realization of one's own freedom, but is instead a question of interplay between autonomy and interdependence. A human being is, as Ruth C. Cohn – who will be discussed in detail in the next chapter – states, more autonomous in realizing his/her freedom the more he/she is aware of his/her relatedness.[16]

Particularly in modern times, there have been many attempts to reject the relationship of humankind to God, the conditionality of our freedom in God's will and our God-given human dignity, and to replace these with autonomous, self-made laws. According to Annemarie Pieper, many of these conceptions are lacking in, for example, sensitivity to the social, as mentioned by Friedrich Nietzsche, and, thus, to the relatedness of humankind.[17]

Finally, with regard to the issues relating to freedom discussed so far, we can conclude by agreeing with Andreas Renz's view that there is no 'essential difference'[18] between the positions of Islam and Christianity on this subject.

Reason as the Ability to Create Relationships

We use the word 'reason' to describe the ability to determine the relationship between good and evil, deal with freedom and relatedness, and bring freedom and relatedness into an appropriate relationship. Reason enables and performs the classification of that which we encounter into the total context that determines freedom. These are continuous acts of further and new determination. However, reason should not take on a life of its own, as has frequently happened in our traditions. Since it is characterized on the basis of experiences and the previously known regulatory

---

16   Cohn, Ruth C., and Farau, Alfred, *Gelebte Geschichte der Psychotherapie. Zwei Perspektiven*. Stuttgart 2008, 357.
17   See Pieper, Annemarie, Riskante Freiheit. Der Hang zum Bösen und seine Folgen. In: Lindenau, Mathias, and Meier Kressig, Marcel (eds.), *Was ist der Mensch? Vier ethische Betrachtungen* (Vadian Lectures, Vol. 1). Bielefeld 2015, 51–70, 63.
18   See Renz, *Der Mensch unter dem An-Spruch Gottes*, 411.

framework, it is a matter of perspective.[19] At the same time, humankind is challenged, by means of reason, to reflect, if necessary, to redefine this regulatory framework. The confrontation with evaluations and boundaries is part of the task of the rational-minded human being.

The scriptures of both religions reveal that reason is an essential human characteristic that performs proportionality determinations, expresses relatedness and creates relationships. Thus, reason is a prerequisite for communication. From a theological point of view, it enables people to communicate with God, fellow human beings and the natural environment. This empowerment enables people not only to receive the divine message passively, but also to allow themselves to be addressed, to respond, and to take part in shaping it. This communication is not limited to the relationship of individuals to God, but also extends to their relationship to the community of human beings. Thus, people are challenged to communicate with each other, to gain new insights and to make themselves useful to all for a good life.[20] The Qur'an encourages people to use reason. In the Bible, there is little explicit discussion of reason; there is more discussion of understanding, insight, and so on. By analogy, one could understand the createdness of humankind as an image of God (Gen. 1:27) and the commissioning of humankind to the care for life and the world (Gen. 1:28) as an assignment to use our reason in order to make possible a good life for all creatures. By reason or reasonable action, the Bible understands above all the orientation of life toward God or actions that are directed toward God. Therefore, biblically, there is frequently no distinction made between reason and faith.[21]

From a Muslim point of view, the relationship between reason and faith must not be torn apart. Therefore, in the realm of faith, it is important to rely on rational arguments and not to construct an opposition between reason and faith, even though reason cannot fully exploit faith.[22]

19   See, in this regard, Kurt Wuchterl's conception of contingency from, as explained in 'What if It Were Completely Different?' in Chapter 4.
20   See Qur'an: 2:164, 39:9, 2:44, 59:2.
21   See Schellenberg, Annette, Vernunft/Verstand (AT). Internet resource: <https://www.bibelwissenschaft.de/stichwort/34095/> [accessed on January 30, 2017].
22   See Ibn Rushd, *Maßgebliche Abhandlung. Faṣl al-maqāl*. Berlin 2010.

Furthermore, it should be noted that reason is not reduced exclusively to the cognitive dimension, that is, the mind, but rather embraces the whole of the life orientation and in this sense corresponds to freedom, wisdom, insight, and responsibility.

Responsibility as the 'Counterbalance' to the Use of Freedom

Responsibility is the consequence of the appropriate use of reason. It represents the relationship of people to themselves, to others and to creation as a whole and to the Creator. Responsibility is not an obstacle to freedom, but rather its relatedness-oriented implementation.

According to the Islamic understanding, the responsibility of the human being is linked to his/her fundamental anthropological conditions, such as free will, his/her status as God's deputy on earth, and the capacity for self-reflection. The special position of humankind within creation means that humankind has a particular responsibility. In this sense, the responsibility of humankind is a natural consequence of our being, which, among other things, is characterized by the fact that God made creation available to us. As Kenneth Cragg rightly emphasizes, this peculiarity of humankind implies both 'domination' and 'submission.'[23] From a Muslim perspective, this interdependence has enormous significance, especially in the context of human freedom, since it demonstrates that the privilege of humankind is closely linked to our responsibility toward all of creation. Therefore, human freedom must not be understood as an unrestricted sovereignty over creation, which would imply arbitrary action. In this regard, the Qur'an verse 'So does man, then, think that it is up to him to act according to his will?' (31:20) alludes to the fact that human beings are not unrestricted in their freedom and must take care of God's creation in order to do justice to God's trust.

23 See Cragg, Kenneth, *The Privilege of Man. A theme in Judaism, Islam and Christianity*. London 1968, 24. Cragg states: 'Man is the condition of all values because they have been rooted in his response. This gives him at once both mastery and subordination: he is defining and de-fined with the real, achiever and achieved. The trust by which he commands is he stature in which he is tributary.'

Thus, from an Islamic point of view, the whole of creation is to be understood as an entrustment (*Amana*) from God, through which God gives humankind temporally limited authority over creation, but expects from us responsible dealings, for which we must ultimately be held accountable before God.[24]

Gen. 2:15 addresses the responsibility that humankind has for creation. God expects that humankind will care of it. This is also expected of the Old Testament kings: Not ruling over, but caring for the entrusted, is the command of God (see, inter alia, Deut. 17:4–20).

Luke 15:1–32 also addresses this responsibility. In this context, it is about the responsibility for the lost, that is, those on the wrong path. The examples given are the shepherd who pursues his sheep until he finds it; the woman who persistently seeks her drachma; and, finally, the merciful father who does not give up on his son, but instead looks for him every day and lovingly receives him when he returns in repentance. Conversely, some biblical texts, such as Matt. 25:14–30, deal with what happens when humankind does not perceive his responsibility. In Luke 16:10–12, we find further statements about the handling of entrusted goods and the reliability humankind should demonstrate even in relation to small things.

In sum, God-given human dignity plays a central role in the context of createdness. Human dignity can only be realized under the conditions of freedom. Freedom, however, is ambivalent and can be used appropriately or it can be misused. The principle that – for religious people in the sight of God – guides proper dealings with people and the proper use of goods is designated as responsibility. In both the Islamic and the Christian contexts, responsibility is closely linked with the concern for God's creation and the execution of God's mission.

Humanity under the Conditions of Concrete Current Contexts

When we remember the contexts in which we find ourselves today and focus on concrete people in their religious ideological constitutions, we become aware that the basic anthropological assumptions appear idealistic

---

24   See Sejdini, Armutsbekämpfung und Gerechtigkeit aus islamischer Perspektive, 298.

and our contextual realities seem, from time to time, far removed from them. We must recognize that human dignity is being trampled on and that people are being deprived of their liberty, with the result that the realization of responsibility is difficult. This applies to violent contexts of all kinds, as well as to the refugee movements, in which the bare minimum necessary for survival is available. It is clear that only a comparatively small elite has the appropriate latitude for the use of freedom and responsibility.

In this context of the suppression and denial of freedom and responsibility, religions and religious communities play a significant role. Examples of this include defining human dignity based on one's own person and group, opposing accusations and settlements of injustices by religious communities, opposing claims of domination with regard to life and ways of life, disregarding human rationality in favor of religious ideologies, or fending off secularity and plurality. We also find many examples of exclusionary and therefore violent effects in our everyday language and in our everyday categorizations. Last but not least, religion, and the categorizations associated with it – as indicated above – can contribute to this.[25]

Violent claims are made not only by the religious communities, but also by groups with other worldviews, including secular or secularistic and atheistic worldviews, which ascribe the cause of violence primarily to religions or want to ban religion from the public domain.

Overall, it has become clear that fundamental and concrete empirical perspectives in religious pedagogical and religious didactic research must be investigated in relation to each other. This is a prerequisite for working in an interreligious manner.

How Do We Understand 'God and the World'?

In the previous section, humanity was considered from a religious theological perspective. We will now deal with the question of how we, as Muslim and Christian religious pedagogues, can understand God and the world and

25 See Lingen-Ali and Mecheril, Religion als soziale Deutungspraxis, 17.

talk about it. In doing so, theology is a viable bridge. Considering that in the two religions there is not just *one* theology, but rather that theology is multifarious, both our specific theological understanding and our perspectives on theology must be generally determined. The content of this determination depends on how we understand the relationship between God and the world and how we approach the question of God in terms of content. It is also possible to determine the question of God devoid of context and biography, so to speak, with little reference to reality or practice. However, this does not correspond with our concern and our understanding of theology, which situates the question of God in the midst of people's lives.

A 'Worldly' and Empathic Theology

If theology is situated in the midst of people's lives, then real humanity, in all its forms and with all its challenges, inherent dilemmas and aporias, belongs to man. A world-oriented and empathic theology takes into consideration the individual in his or her comprehensive relatedness, as well as the interaction and the communication and the context. In the process, it does not avoid thematizing injustices, constructed asymmetries, power relations and dependency strategies. It inquires into those 'generative issues'[26] that deeply affect people and the world. In this sense, theology is never monologically related to the scientific understanding of traditions. In its basic intention, it is dialogic;[27] in other words, it is focused on the ever-changing understanding of 'God in the world.' In dealing with different theological understandings, the following questions arise: What status do the biographical, the social and the contextual have for a theological concept? Which methodology is inscribed in a theological concept? Does it relate to a static-instructional approach, or the process-oriented forms into which current life situations and perspectives are

---

26 The term 'generative themes' is used both by the Brazilian liberation pedagogue Paulo Freire, as well as by the founder of Theme-Centered Interaction (TCI), Ruth C. Cohn. A detailed explanation of the term can be found in the third chapter.
27 See Khorchide, Mouhanad, *Islam der Barmherzigkeit. Grundzüge einer modernen Religion* (Herder Spektrum, Vol. 6764). Freiburg i. Br. 2015.

vividly interwoven together with the findings of the traditions and in which truth is only ever recognized fragmentarily and never reveals itself absolutely, but instead out of context and process?

A theology that aims exclusively at the systematization of knowledge of God and the world and that does not sufficiently consider biography, relationships, or contexts can be found in most of the religious traditions. In a deliberate effort to avoid this, our concept identifies an implicit–explicit access to theology that assumes that theology and theologizing take place not only on an 'upscale' scientific level, but also in communication 'among ourselves.' Such an approach considers the entire world, the dynamics of our relationships, the debate within the individual, and the conflicts in context to be theologically relevant and attempts to explicitly translate what is already implicit into theological language.

When we pursue the goal of creating an authentic interreligious religious pedagogy and religious didactics 'on equal terms,' the conception of theology we hold to be binding is not insignificant, for this essentially shapes our concepts, our forms of action and our togetherness. Therefore, it is necessary to take a closer look at the central theological notions, such as the concept of God and the understanding of revelation.

God as the Absolutely Different

Just as there are different concepts of theology, so there are different conceptions of God. Thus, a person might say that he has adequately grasped God, faith, and theology when he observes everything correctly and has learned everything there is to learn about God. Others believe that God can never be fully comprehended. The latter is articulated using different metaphors and analogies: God as the absolutely different; God as the incomprehensible in human thought and language; God as an inexpressible secret, etc.

When God is understood as the absolutely different, the not entirely comprehensible, the unavailable, then God is not directly and immediately accessible to theology, but is instead accessible only through traces and signs in the world, to which the scriptures of the religions (in our case the

Bible and the Qur'an) bear witness. Christians and Muslims perceive the central figures of their faith, Jesus and Muhammad, as the specific 'exegetes' in their respective sacred traditions, who became for the believers a model for their relationship to God. However, Christians differ from Muslims in that, for them, the ineffable mystery of God took on an earthly form in Jesus Christ and thus God became tangible in a concrete human being.

When Muslims and Christians reflect on God, they exhibit very different understandings of the representability of God. Christians are often tempted to create 'pictures' or ideas of God that are far too concrete. This is prevented by the Jewish and Muslim prohibition of images. In spite of such prohibition, which was also the subject of heated debate in Christianity,[28] the fact that all people have an idea or understanding (and, in this sense, an image) of God must not be overlooked.

It is of religious pedagogical significance that these understandings or images are not neutral and objective, but instead represent a mixture of religious theological insights and psychic transmissions. From the point of view of religious psychology, it is imperative that people (consciously or unconsciously) create ideas and images of God for themselves. From a religious pedagogical perspective, therefore, the question of how we can deal with this in an appropriate manner arises. The work on or with these ideas and images represents an important religious pedagogical challenge. Thus, in the dialogue of our two traditions, it is revealed that humankind finds itself in the tension between these images, which it makes, or even inevitably must make, when thinking about God, and the never fully comprehensible and accessible reality of God. This tension is also a great religious didactic challenge. To acknowledge the unavailability of God and remain open is one thing. The other challenge in the religious didactic task is to teach so much about God that people are able to enter into a

---

28 The representability or non-representability of God (Ex. 20:4) was a recurrent thematic matter in Christianity as well. At times, depictions of God were forbidden, then they were allowed again. In the Byzantine Empire, during the time of Emperor Leo III (d. 741), there was a massive prohibition of images. The Second Council of Nicea (787), however, allowed images and their worship. During the Reformation, debates about the prohibition of images flared up again. For Luther, depictions of God and the saints were an abomination.

relationship with God. Whether such a relationship can be established or even succeed in the face of the unavailability of God is not dependent on the efforts of religious pedagogues alone, but also on the trust that God offers and on His actions.

The intensive examination of the question of God has inevitably led to the emergence of various ideas of God among Muslims also, which cannot be discussed here in detail. What seems important in this context, however, is the fact that no dissent exists among Muslims in some key areas. An important common ground in the context of the conception of God is Sura 112:1–5, which states: 'Say: He is the One God; God the Eternal, the uncaused Cause of All That Exists, He begets not and neither is He begotten, and there is nothing that could be compared with Him.'[29] The Sura describes some of God's most important attributes, which give people the opportunity to form some idea of what God is like. Other valuable clues about the known attributes of God are provided by the '99 beautiful names.' The true nature of God, however, eludes human cognition, since, as previously mentioned, nothing like Him is known to human beings. Muslims are therefore encouraged to think more about the signs (*ayat*) of God, as a way of understanding Him, than about His nature, which is inaccessible to humans in any case.[30]

Similar considerations also exist in the Bible and in Christian theology. Thus, we find, among other things, references to the hiddenness of God by the prophet Isaiah ('Truly, you are a hidden God' [Isa. 45:15]), in the psalms of lamentation (Ps. 30, Ps. 51, Ps. 89), in the Gospel of John ('No one has ever seen God' [John 1:18]), and in the letter of the apostle Paul to the Corinthians ('Now we look in a mirror and see only enigmatic outlines, but then we look face to face' [1 Cor. 13:12]). In the Christian theological tradition, we find the central idea of 'negative theology'[31] regarding the unknowability of God and consequently the view that the nature of God

---

29 Asad, *The Message of the Qur'an*, 1124.
30 See Schimmel, Annemarie, *Die Zeichen Gottes. Die religiöse Welt des Islam*. Munich 1995, 150.
31 See Halbmayr, Alois, and Hafner Johann, *Negative Theologie heute? Zum aktuellen Stellenwert einer umstrittenen Tradition*. Freiburg i. Br. 2008.

can never be adequately grasped in human language, or, in other words, that one can only state what God is not.

Despite divergent conceptions of God, there is a basic consensus in both religions that the nature of God ultimately remains hidden from us. Thus, all statements about God are subject to fundamental reservation. The fact that God is unavailable in His nature determines the way in which people communicate with God and vice versa. Therefore, in the next section we wish to clarify which understanding of revelation underlies our concept.

Understanding of Revelation: How Does God Communicate With Us Humans?

The question of how God communicates with people and how He manifests Himself is a central theme of both religions. The special position of humankind in creation has made us God's contact on earth. At the same time, we must be aware that communication with or from God is different to that of people among themselves.

If we nevertheless speak of a communicative event in connection with revelation, the question arises, first of all, of how people relate to God and how they can address Him. On the one hand, one can ask how God communicates and how He wants to be addressed.

From a Catholic perspective, until the Second Vatican Council (1962–1965), access to revelation was largely information- and instruction-theoretical. In certain circles, this approach is still widespread even today, in case, for example, the catechism is understood as a normative book that summarizes the essentials of the doctrines of faith in an exclusively content-oriented manner.

The question of divine revelation and its character is by and large an issue that gained its explosiveness only in the confrontation with the Enlightenment and the emerging (natural) sciences and was formulated from the Catholic perspective in the First Vatican Council (1869–1870). A 'natural' religion and ever more differentiated human knowledge are juxtaposed with knowledge that is not accessible through reason. God reveals himself in this understanding not only in 'natural' ways in which man can recognize God in creation, for example, with the help of his reason, but also in another, supernatural way, which fundamentally transcends human reason. In the traditional conception of revelation, which, from the Catholic perspective, prevailed until the Second Vatican Council, it is divine knowledge that comes to humankind from the outside, through revelation, and is taught, true and authentic, in the doctrine of the Catholic Church.

The texts of the Second Vatican Council take up the doctrine of revelation; in this way, they follow in the footsteps of the previous councils. But the intention with which they speak of revelation, and the form in which they deal with it, fundamentally changed. For the first time in the history of the Church, an entire Council document, *Dei Verbum* [Word of God], is dedicated exclusively to revelation. The Catholic Church, or dogmatics, became more aware of the historicity of their claims to truth. It consciously opened itself up to the 'world' as a place of theological knowledge. The theological confrontation with the 'signs of the times'[32] became, in this context, a binding mandate of the Church. Revelation as the 'word of God' is understood as a communication event whose purpose is not to communicate to man only certain truths that are unknowable by means of reason, but rather to address people in all dimensions of their existence and to lead them to salvation. The revelation is God's devotion and self-communication to humankind, who is invited to communion with Him and with each other. God addresses humans 'as friends' and 'associates with them.'[33] According to the understanding of the Second Vatican Council, revelation is thus a living process, in which humankind is involved as a 'hearer of the word'[34] in a personal dialogue.

In this sense, the Christian form of revelation is not an abundance of abstract truths to defend against other religions, but rather an encounter with a concrete historical man, Jesus of Nazareth, whom Christians bear witness to as Christ. The 'Word of God hath become flesh' (John 1:14) and

---

32 Zweites Vatikanisches Konzil, *Pastorale Konstitution über die Kirche in der Welt von heute Gaudium et spes*, Nr. 4.
33 Zweites Vatikanisches Konzil, *Dogmatische Konstitution über die göttliche Offenbarung Dei Verbum*, Nr. 2.
34 See Rahner, Karl, *Hörer des Wortes. Zur Grundlegung einer Religionsphilosophie*. Freiburg i. Br. 1971.

Jesus Christ is 'at the same time mediator and the fullness of the whole revelation.'[35]

According to M. Thurner, the very Christological centering of Christian revelation, which departs from the exclusivism of Catholic truth and requires enlivening through action and living, opens the way for the acknowledgment of God's revelation in other religions: 'Wherever people are led to their salvation, revelation happens as God's promise of salvation.'[36]

As in all revelatory religions, revelation[37] also plays an important role in Islam. Driven by the idea that the revelations of earlier religions deviated from their original form due to human influences, Islamic theology places special emphasis on the authenticity of the Qur'an, which is understood by Muslims to be the literal revelation of God.

The central position of the revelation, or the Qur'an, as the verbal inspiration of God, which is often compared to the position of Jesus in Christianity, led to the implementation of a rather static revelatory understanding within Islamic theology. Such a static understanding can, however, have serious consequences. In the Islamic context, the impact of this understanding of revelation was such that it was supposed that the Qur'an was recorded on 'well-preserved tablets'[38] before it was gradually revealed to the Prophet Muhammad over a 23-year period. This view led to a very harsh discussion within Islam about whether the Qur'an was created or uncreated.[39]

---

35 Zweites Vatikanisches Konzil, *Dei Verbum*, Nr. 2.
36 Thurner, Martin, Von der Information zur Kommunikation. Das Offenbarungsverständnis der beiden Vatikanischen Konzilien. In: Heinzmann, Richard, and Selçuk, Mualla (eds.), *Offenbarung in Christentum und Islam* (Interkulturelle und interreligiöse Symposien der Eugen-Biser-Stiftung, Vol. 5). Stuttgart 2011, 129–143.
37 In this context, it is important to point out that the meaning of the term 'revelation' in the Christian context only partially corresponds to the Muslim pendant *al-wahy*. Revelation as *wahy* in the classical sense is limited to the divine communication with the Prophet.
38 See Qur'an, 85:22.
39 See Khoury, Adel Theodor (trans.), *Der Koran*. Band 1. Sure 1:1–2,74. Gütersloh 1990, 99.

The adoption of a literal, context-free and normative approach to the Qur'anic text has become established particularly in fundamentalist circles, leading, on the one hand, to stagnation and, on the other hand, to the reduction of the revelation of God to a book.[40]

The Muslim scholar Abu Zaid contradicts this position. Based on the Qur'an verses 18:109 and 31:27, in which it is stated that neither the transformation of all trees into writing instruments, nor the seas into ink, would suffice to exhaust the comprehensive Word of God, he is of the opinion that the Qur'an can only be a 'particular manifestation of the Word of God.'[41]

Accordingly, the understanding of revelation should be broader if the revelation of God is to serve as a guidance for all times. The Qur'an also indicates the signs of God and urges human beings to use their mind to be inspired by the signs of God.[42] In this context, the Qur'an states:

> Verily, in the creation of the heavens and of the earth and the succession of night and day; in the ships that speed through the sea with what is useful to man; and in the waters that God sends down from the sky, giving life thereby to the earth after it had been lifeless, and causing all manner of living creatures to multiply thereon; and in the change of the winds, and the clouds that run their appointed courses between sky and earth; [in all this] there are messages indeed for those who use their reason. (2:164)[43]

The greatest challenge facing Islamic theology lies in the transformation of the understanding of revelation from an instructional, informational approach, with a claim to objective knowledge transfer, to a dialogic, communicative approach, which can serve as a guide to those Muslims who believe in taking the contexts of revelation into consideration. Only through such a transformation can the revelation have a positive effect on people in spite of the temporal distance between the time of its origin and the present, for the sacred text remains, as Rotraud Wieland accurately formulated, 'revelation

---

40 See Sejdini, Zwischen Gewissheit und Kontingenz, 25.
41 See Abū-Zaid, Naṣr Ḥāmid, *Gottes Menschenwort. Für ein humanistisches Verständnis des Koran*. Freiburg i. Br. 2008, 126.
42 See Renz, Andreas, Die 'Zeichen Gottes' (ayat Allah). Sakramentalität im Islam und ihre Bedeutung für das christlich-islamische Verhältnis. In: *Theologische Zeitschrift* (2005), 239–257.
43 Asad, *The Message of the Qur'an*, 43.

only as long as people are convinced that they can benefit by believing in what it says and by doing what it commands. Otherwise, it will not reveal anything, but instead is only of historical interest.'[44]

It is clear from what has been said so far that, despite differences in emphases and influences, there are similarities in how Christians and Muslims understand revelation. With regard to the current religious pedagogical and religious didactic challenges, a communication-oriented understanding of revelation that takes human experience into account is inevitable. Thus, exploring, from a religious pedagogical theological perspective, human contexts and living conditions, with regard to the revelation of God, becomes central. Human contexts and living conditions are the points of departure for the revelation. They have challenged it and given it concrete shape. What people have experienced throughout time, and are still experiencing today, unfolds and differentiates the revelation.

God, in his revelation to mankind, is concerned to express himself according to the possibilities of the addressees. This leads to linguistic, cultural and historical contingency. Seen in this way, revelation is not an end in itself, but an ongoing, possibility-oriented and living event that creates new horizons for a good life for all and everything.

For this to be effective, we must ask ourselves which approach we must adopt, under religious pedagogical and religious didactic consideration, so that the revelation can be opened up to us on that basis, as well as what opportunities we leave unused, if we do not take that approach.

Theology as Science from a Religious Pedagogical Perspective

In the preceding reflections on man, God and the world, religious pedagogical contexts became increasingly visible. They will now be addressed in their specific theological scientific context. The question arises as to

---

44 Wielandt, Rotraud, *Offenbarung und Geschichte im Denken moderner Muslime*. Wiesbaden 1971, 2–4.

the location of religious pedagogy in the context of theology against the background of certain scientific understandings. A theology, which starts from religious pedagogical questions, has to deal with experience and thus with subject and context orientation.

For such an understanding of theology, several levels of language are relevant: speech to God (e.g. in prayer), speech from God as a reflection on specific human experiences, speech about God, as a more rationally influenced and logically argued insight, and the speech of God Himself as the revelation of God.

Furthermore, the question of the specific attributes of theology arises in the scientific theoretical theological context. This is frequently associated with a purely substantive material understanding. That is, the theological is understood as a clearly circumscribable and explicitly religious subject area, such as, for example, the content of faith, explicitly theological concepts, religious rites, the actions of the church or religious community, etc. Such an understanding is too concise from the point of view of an experience-oriented religious pedagogy, since, according to this point of view, the theological is present more in one's perspective on something. Thus, it is the 'formal object,' the consideration, which makes up the theological. This consideration also delimits theology from other sciences, and therefore a theologically oriented religious pedagogy from an educational science–oriented pedagogy. By taking such an approach, the objects of possible theological consideration are broadened: It is no longer exclusively religiously connoted objects that can be theologically reflected, but rather, in principle, everything.[45] For

---

45 See here the approach of Roman Siebenrock, in the context of the course entitled Theory of Science II in the Cath.-Theological Department Innsbruck. See, in that regard: Forschungskreis Kommunikative Theologie/Communicative Theology Research Group (ed.), *Kommunikative Theologie. Selbstvergewisserung unserer Kultur des Theologietreibens/Communicative Theology. Reflections on the Culture of Our Practice of Theology* (Kommunikative Theologie – interdisziplinär/ Communicative Theology – Interdisciplinary Studies, Vol. 1). Vienna 2007, 80; see also: Ziebertz, Hans-Georg, Religionspädagogik und empirische Methodologie. In: Schweitzer, Friedrich, and Schlag, Thomas (eds.), *Religionspädagogik im 21. Jahrhundert. Herausforderungen und Zukunftsperspektiven*. Gütersloh/Freiburg i. Br. 209–222, 221.

the field of education, this means that while there is a particular expectation regarding religious education processes, all other educational processes can nevertheless be the subject of a theologically aligned religious pedagogy. This is exemplified by Maria Juen's dissertation.[46] The subject of her qualitative empirical investigation is not only the initial minutes of a lesson in religious education, but also the initial minutes of lessons in physics and mathematics instruction. In this way, the phenomenon of the beginning of a lesson in the most varied subjects is regarded as a theological space and subjected to theological religious pedagogical reflections.

We have just made a formal definition of the theological. When it comes to the contentual orientation, the question of God is at the center of theological attention. It stands (implicitly or explicitly) in the background of any theological, and thus also of any religious pedagogical, debate. The question of God can assume different shapes in terms of content, depending on how God is addressed or how we believe that he can be addressed: Sometimes, for example, God is addressed as the ultimate cause of all being, or as the ultimate goal that can be pursued for its own sake, as the highest form of bliss, as the unavailable, as the guarantor of hope for new possibilities, and so on and so forth. However, the way in which the question of God is determined in terms of content always has to do with the question of man and his situation. The question of God is concerned therefore with a theology that is tied to being human and that does not exclusively have the teaching, doctrine or tradition of faith in view, but also focuses on the human being with his needs, longings and hopes. One consequence of this is that the goal of theology should be the good life for all people.

So far, we have talked about the subject and the perspective of theology or a theologically oriented religious pedagogy. No less important are the epistemological orientation and the forms of knowledge acquisition in the sense of a methodology. We understand theology as a science that cannot count on 'safe ground' and 'secure houses.' It must not take the place of the

---

46 Juen, Maria, *Die ersten Minuten des Unterrichts. Skizzen einer Kairologie des Anfangs aus kommunikativ-theologischer Perspektive*. Münster 2013.

truths of faith and should always understand knowledge as temporary. In this sense, theology could be characterized more by a questioning scientific nature and – as Fritz Simon formulated it – should be aware of the fact that knowledge limits the sense of possibility.[47]

Despite all these particularities, theology is challenged to face the scientific standards of other sciences. The danger of theology is often that one will lose sight of the limited objectivity, which must be striven for despite all subjectivity and provisionality. Theology must always ensure that its scientific character is maintained, especially as regards comprehensibility and intersubjective verifiability of findings and results.[48]

How Do We Understand the Concept of Education?

In addition to the anthropological and theological approaches, one's understanding of education is also one of the foundations of interreligious religious pedagogy and religious didactics. This raises the question of how we understand the term 'education' and how it relates to what we discussed earlier.

On the one hand, the notion of education is invoked in relation to politics, society and the economy and is often used in an inflated manner, as a result of which it becomes meaningless. On the other hand, by focusing on the concept of learning and competence, there is a risk of narrowing down and reducing the concept of education. This should be avoided, particularly in the context of interreligious religious pedagogy and religious didactics, by giving the concept of education new attention. In doing so, we assume a broad, multi-layered and process-oriented understanding of education that includes one's own self, one's relationship with others, an

---

47 See Simon, Fritz, *Die Kunst nicht zu lernen und andere Paradoxien in Psychotherapie, Management, Politik*. Heidelberg 1999, 133; 157.
48 See Schärtl, Thomas, *Wahrheit und Gewissheit. Zur Eigenart religiösen Glaubens*. Kevelaer 2004, 164.

examination of what education entails, the objective content and the surrounding context.⁴⁹

With regard to interreligiosity, understandings of education that are relationship-oriented and that deal with the other are essential. Rainer Kokemohr understands education as 'a process [...] which is triggered by an unfamiliar demand.'⁵⁰ In the context of education, the idea of the 'border' comprises something similar: Education occurs in the process of stepping out, in opening up, in daring, in encounters and relationships with other people and in letting others take advantage of what one has to offer. Wherever we reach limits is where we are confronted with the unfamiliar, the unknown, the unavailable and the uncertain.⁵¹ In this case, contradiction and resistance increase, making one's own blind spots visible. Above all, such engagement makes 'formative experiences' possible.⁵² Henning Luther, quoting Paul Tillich, describes the border as 'the actual fertile place of knowledge.'⁵³

Education as Formation

The origin of the German word for education is credited to the mystic Meister Eckhart, who took as a starting point a divinely formed center

---

49   See, in this regard: Lederer, Bernd, *Kompetenz oder Bildung? Eine Analyse jüngerer Konnotationsverschiebungen des Bildungsbegriffs und Plädoyer für eine Rück- und Neubesinnung auf ein transinstrumentelles Bildungsverständnis.* Innsbruck 2012, 309–311.
50   Kokemohr, Rainer, Bildung als Welt- und Selbstentwurf im Anspruch des Fremden. In: Koller, Hans-Christoph, Marotzki, Winfried, and Sanders, Olaf (eds.), *Bildungsprozesse und Fremdheitserfahrung. Beiträge zu einer Theorie transformatorischer Bildungsprozesse.* Bielefeld 2007, 13–68, 14.
51   See Kraml, Martina, Grenzgänge. In: Scharer, Matthias, and Kraml, Martina (eds.), *Vom Leben herausgefordert. Praktisch-theologisches Forschen als kommunikativer Prozess.* Mainz 2003, 159–179.
52   Schratz, Michael, Schwarz, Johanna, and Westfall-Greiter, Tanja, *Lernen als bildende Erfahrung. Vignetten in der Praxisforschung.* Innsbruck 2012.
53   Luther, Henning, *Religion und Alltag. Bausteine einer Praktischen Theologie des Subjekts.* Stuttgart 1992, 60.

in man, which was to be discovered by 'removing' all external images (unforming; German term: *Entbildung*).[54]

In a broader sense, education is understood as *formatio* [formation], or *transformatio* [transformation], in the Western tradition. These terms are usually translated into German as '*Formung*' [forming], '*Gestaltung*' [shaping], '*Gestaltgebung*' [giving shape to], or '*Umgestaltung*' [transformation].[55] In this sense, education can be understood as the process that gives shape to the basic anthropological and theological orientations. In other words, in education, the question of being human and the question of life orientation acquire their form or their shape, from the perspective of religious pedagogy, but also in the sense of religious orientation. Thus, Rudolf Englert speaks of a 'vision, of "true", "successful" being human,' which should be brought into 'form' by means of education.[56] This means that the concept of education always encompasses an examination of the normative foundations of life and coexistence, which are reflected in the following questions: Which visions and which ideas should be manifested and shaped in which educational processes, educational institutions and educational policy concepts? How do they relate to being human? How compatible are they with human dignity? Or, posed differently: What form does education take in our societal, economic, and religious-community context, and, from a theological religious pedagogical perspective, are there compatibilities or incompatibilities with being human in the context of freedom and justice?

54 See Meyer-Drawe, Käte, 'Du sollst dir kein Bildnis noch Gleichnis machen ...' – Bildung und Versagung. In: Koller, Marotzki and Sanders (eds.), *Bildungsprozesse und Fremdheitserfahrung*, 83–94, 88.
55 See Meyer-Drawe Käte, Entbildung – Einbildung – Bildung. Zur Bedeutung der Imago-Die-Lehre für moderne Bildungstheorien. In: Behrens, Rudolf (ed.), *Ordnungen des Imaginären. Theorien der Imagination in funktionsgeschichtlicher Zeit*. Hamburg 2001, 181–194, 184; 187. See also: Schambeck, Mirjam, 'Weil es um den Menschen geht, wenn wir von Bildung reden ...' – Religionspädagogische Einmischungen zur Debatte um Bildungsstandards. In: Sajak, Clauß Peter (ed.), *Bildungsstandards für den Religionsunterricht*. Berlin 2007, 179–202, 186.
56 Englert, Rudolf, *Religionspädagogische Grundfragen. Anstöße zur Urteilsbildung*. Stuttgart 2007, 11.

These questions, in our view, demonstrate the indispensability and added value of the theological perspective. God can be understood as the one who relativizes human power claims, fosters autonomy, and thus is the steadfast guarantor of non-purposeful and therefore humane education. In this respect, life-promoting education must lead to freedom and maturity. An uneducated person who has not exposed himself/herself to, or has not been exposed to, 'borderline' encounters and disputes, can easily be 'coded' and manipulated so that independent thinking and justification of one's own actions wither away or even cannot occur.[57] In contrast, and with reference to the understanding of God of which we have spoken, an education with a religious theological claim should lead a person to be able to shape his or her relationship with himself/herself, with others, and with the whole context (in the language of theme-centered interaction: the 'Globe') more reflectively, responsibly and freely.[58] At this point, there is a link to the understanding of creation, in which we have addressed createdness, freedom, reason, and responsibility, and placed them in relation to each other.

Religious Education in the Context of the Immigration Society

Education and educational work in the most varied fields of action are always context-dependent and politically determined. In particular, refugee and immigration movements, such as we described in Chapter 1, characterize the Central European context. As religious pedagogues, we do not therefore have to reflect on concepts and practices – in their objectified context – as, for example, philosophers often do. As has already been emphasized, it is also important to critically examine the practical political side and thus the effects and impacts of the concepts and

---

57 See Arendt, Hannah, *Eichmann in Jerusalem. Ein Bericht von der Banalität des Bösen*. Munich 2011, 56f.

58 This view of theological education contains a high claim, which can be dangerous if it is functionalized. Every human, but especially religious communities as representatives of this perspective, must constantly deal with this claim and reflect his or their individual actions against this background.

practices. Particularly in the context of immigration society, a number of asymmetrical relationships become apparent: The view is most often directed from the majority society toward the immigrants, resulting in a kind of 'one-way street.' There is talk of a 'majority society' and 'locals,' and it is unclear how one should designate the other side: minority society, foreigners, immigrants, etc. Furthermore, members of the majority society often use taken-for-granted distinctions and categorizations in everyday life with hardly any knowledge of their problematic communicative effect in political and social terms.

An important task of education in the various fields of action is therefore to critically reflect on the communicative impact of differentiations or systems of distinctions due to their susceptibility to the construction of asymmetric social relations, in the sense of unjust relationships. Unequal relationships arise, above all, when it is forgotten that distinctions are commonly constructed, that is, in the broadest sense, 'agreed-upon' speech acts. With regard to this oblivion, one often speaks of a 'naturalization' and 'ontologization'[59] of distinctions. This means that fabricated differences or attributions are considered to be natural occurrences, irrefutable or divinely ordained reality. In this way, the relativity of distinctions and categorizations is concealed. In this absolutization lies the power of interpretation, especially regarding educational and teaching and learning contexts. Analyzing the use of language, and reflecting on and critically questioning categorizations, is one of the tasks of interreligious religious pedagogy and religious didactics.

Theory and Practice of Religious Education: Religious Pedagogy and Religious Didactics

In this last section on the topic of understanding education, we want to take a look at the scientific dimension of education or religious education

---

59 See Yildiz, Safiye, *Interkulturelle Erziehung und Pädagogik. Subjektivierung und Macht in den Ordnungen des nationalen Diskurses*. Wiesbaden 2009, 37. See also: Yildiz, Erol, Postmigrantische Perspektiven. Von der Hegemonie zur urbanen Alltagspraxis. In: Doğmuş, Aysun, Karakaşoğlu, Yasemin, and Mecheril, Paul (eds.), *Pädagogisches Können in der Migrationsgesellschaft*. Wiesbaden 2016, 71–82, 71.

and formulate our approaches to religious pedagogy, religious didactics and teaching methodology.

Religious Pedagogy

The ambivalence out of which Christian religious pedagogy emerged is striking. The Christian, above all Catholic, religious pedagogy is more aligned with the tradition of the Enlightenment, or post-Enlightenment, and often adopts a skeptical attitude toward ecclesiastical catechesis. This in turn leads to the Christian faith community being skeptical about the religious pedagogy. In addition, in the eyes of some proponents, the religious pedagogy embodies the scientific and thus the more modern variant of the theory of religious education.

As well as the different formation conditions of Islamic and Christian religious pedagogy, we can hold on to the following fact: While the education paradigm addresses the fundamental questions of the formability of the human as subject and various educational contexts, the religious pedagogical paradigm focuses on the scientific context. Within the Christian theological sciences, religious pedagogy and religious didactics have long been seen by the other theological disciplines as applied sciences. According to this view, still prevalent among some theologians, the theological philosophical and biblical historical disciplines gain the essential insights, while religious pedagogy imparts these insights in the most attractive form possible. In this respect, the Islamic context does not differ significantly from the Christian context. In contrast to the development of Christian religious pedagogy, the idea of religious pedagogy as an applied science still prevails in the Islamic sphere. Nevertheless, there are also currents in Islamic religious pedagogy and religious didactics that do not view religious pedagogy as an applied science, thereby initiating new developments.

Contrary to the notion of an applied science, religious pedagogy and religious didactics today, as has already been made clear, mostly understand themselves as theology-generating sciences, which, from their own perspective, make specific contributions to the process of theological knowledge acquisition. The term 'religious pedagogy' signifies the widest spectrum of religious education or education theory. According to our understanding, it is affiliated with an open concept of education, which understands man as a subject that is capable of being educated – and capable of being religiously educated – through communication with other subjects, contexts and religious traditions. Educational or (in a narrower sense) learning, processes can be explicitly understood as intentional religious learning processes.

From a Catholic perspective, religious pedagogy is traditionally associated with the term 'catechetics,' which is expressed in the double designation of relevant professorships at universities, among other things. According to the traditional Catholic view, catechetics concerns theological didactic reflection on the catechesis of the Church, which sees itself as passing on the central contents of faith to children, adolescents and adults with the goal of religious socialization. In Islam, there is no corresponding designation. The term *al-mihal* is used to impart 'truths of faith' in an adapted form to young people and adults. It is a handbook that is intended to offer the most important beliefs and religious rituals, as well as ethical principles, of Islam in an understandable and compact form.[60]

In the context of an information- and instruction-theoretical view of revelation, catechisms were developed for children, who were taught, in question/response format, 'religious truths.' Jürgen Werbick refers to this access as a 'yes/no communication'[61] as it does not allow any possibility for involvement with one's existential condition in the religious education event.

Religious Didactics and Subject Didactics Religion

Since this book refers specifically to a limited area of religious pedagogy, namely religious didactics, and subject didactics for religious education, marking out this area is of primary importance. If one puts religion and didactics together to form one term and speaks of 'religious didactics,' the tension that necessarily accompanies religious didactic thinking and acting becomes apparent: Apart from the fact that religion has always

---

60 See Kelpetin, Hatice, Ilmihal. In: Türkiye Diyanet vakfi (ed.), *İslâm ansiklopedisi. Standardausgabe*. İstanbul 1988, 139–141.
61 See Werbick, Jürgen, *Glaubenlernen aus Erfahrung. Grundbegriffe einer Didaktik des Glaubens*. Munich 1989, 220–222.

been understood as a specific tradition, today not only the great religious traditions, but also spiritualities, ideological religious attitudes and practices, which are no longer linked to the hitherto valid and institutionalized religious traditions, are being considered. What the term 'religion' refers to in religious didactics, or how narrowly or broadly the concept of religion is understood, is unclear from the outset.

In comparison, the concept of didactics as an art and science of teaching and learning seems at first glance to be unproblematic from a worldview point of view because it appears to be neutral. On closer inspection, however, it turns out that didactics and its respective concepts are by no means neutral and unencumbered in ideological terms. In this context, it is precisely the task of religious pedagogy and religious didactics to critically illuminate the ideological implications. For example, the economic-neoliberal impetus is unmistakable in the efficiency, competence and outcome orientation of current didactics and subject didactics.[62] This makes the σχολή (scholé), as a place of leisure and contemplative thinking, a hectic learning institution. Religion and didactics therefore have a fundamentally critical relationship, particularly regarding their respective ideological religious implications.

In the Innsbruck tradition, we understand religious didactics as the art and science of religious teaching and learning in general. Accordingly, religious didactics deals with the intentional teaching and learning in educational institutions from a worldview and religious perspective, but it also deals with worldview relevant questions from didactics. Subject didactics for religion, on the other hand, refers to teaching and learning in the school context, or in the context of religious education at school. Naturally, questions arising from and tensions between religion and didactics come into play in relation to the religious didactic context. School, and school teaching and learning, require constant critical review that centers on an understanding of people and education and includes an articulated or unarticulated reference to transcendence.

---

62 See, among others, Masschelein, Jan, and Simsons, Maarten, *Globale Immunität. Oder eine kleine Kartographie des europäischen Bildungsraums*. Zurich 2012; Liessmann, Konrad Paul, *Geisterstunde. Die Praxis der Unbildung. Eine Streitschrift*. Vienna 2014.

A criticism of the educational institutions, from a religious pedagogical and religious didactic perspective, must never be expressed in a patronizing manner that makes theologians the only experts of the true humanity.[63]

The effects of traditional religious pedagogy and catechetics are ambivalent, because they sometimes reduce children, adolescents and even adults to dependent objects of particular religious convictions and denominations. In this respect, theological religious pedagogical criticism of didactics, schools and other places of learning should always be carried out in an attitude of mutually bearing and sharing the responsibility for human deficits.

Religious education at school, as the most concrete location of action in teaching methodology for religion, is, on the one hand, limited to the critical function of giving the good life for all people a conceivable form, which opens up a viable life path to children and adolescents. On the other hand, religious education at school, as we understand it, also familiarizes them with specific religious traditions in a way that further develops and challenges students' judgment and decision-making abilities.

Through area-covering religious education at school, many religion teachers are engaged in areas of school development. This seems indispensable to the goal of developing humane and just education and educational institutions. In subject didactics, therefore, there are always new ways of working on concrete designs and projects to discover how religion can come to life in schools. This requires models for religious didactics and teaching methodological didactics, such as the Innsbruck model of religious didactics, which is developed further in Chapter 5 with respect to Muslim–Christian cooperation. Many aspects have to be considered: Guiding a class or learning group as a specific challenge for teachers must also be taken into account and practiced, as teaching that stimulates learning, which particularly challenges the teacher, as a central medium, alongside other media. Thereby the issue of professionalization is also addressed. It goes without saying that lessons must be constantly evaluated and planning

---

63   See Scharer, Matthias, Die Schule und das Leben (in Fülle). Religionspädagogische Optionen in der Schulentwicklung. In: Jäggle, Martin, Krobath, Thomas, and Schelander, Robert (eds.), *lebens.werte.schule. Religiöse Dimensionen in Schulkultur und Schulentwicklung*. Vienna 2009, 379–386, 381.

must be revised repeatedly so that learning remains dynamic for students and teachers.

Consequences for an Interreligious Religious Pedagogy and Religious Didactics

Based on the joint work in Chapter 2 on the foundations of an interreligious religious pedagogy and religious didactics, we conclude that reflection on one's own anthropological and theological, as well as educational, concepts is imperative. Possibilities of understanding between us Muslims and Christians arise from such reflection. In our considerations, inner connections between images of man, images of God and understandings of education, which shape the foundations of religious pedagogy and religious didactics, became clear. If one takes the meaning of lifeworld relations and human experiences seriously, theological reflection cannot be introduced exclusively at the expert level. These considerations give rise to the question of the orientations of a quality understanding of education, based on anthropological and theological insights. This knowledge is gathered over the course of this volume and will be explicated in the guidelines of the fifth chapter.

CHAPTER 3

Religious Pedagogy and Religious Didactics: Where Do We Come From?

Appreciation of biographical narratives, attention to the contexts we live in and clarification of the anthropological, theological and religious pedagogical foundations, which we thematized in the preceding chapters, are integral to the way we work in Innsbruck with regard to religious pedagogy and religious didactics. This chapter addresses our religious pedagogical and religious didactic origin, as we would like, on the one hand, to clarify the background of the so-called 'Innsbruck model of religious didactics,' and, on the other hand, to make it fruitful for interreligious religious pedagogy and religious didactics. To make this background easier to grasp, we will begin by discussing the specific foundations of the interreligious religious pedagogy and religious didactics in Innsbruck.

The Background of the Interreligious Religious Pedagogy and Religious Didactics in Innsbruck

The recent history of religious pedagogy and religious didactics at the Catholic Theological Faculty of the University of Innsbruck is influenced in particular by two concepts: Theme-Centered Interaction (TCI), based on the work of Ruth C. Cohn, and Communicative Theology (ComTheo). These are given a concrete religious didactic from in the so-called 'Innsbruck model of religious didactics.'[1] This is characterized by

[1] Scharer, Matthias, Religion unterrichten lernen. Das Innsbrucker Modell. In: Arntz, Anne, and Isenberg, Wolfgang (eds.), *Kompetenz für die Praxis?*

the – deliberate and theologically considered – reception of common religious pedagogical currents, such as correlation and symbol didactics and competence orientation.

Both TCI and ComTheo go beyond narrow (religious) pedagogical issues. TCI is practiced in various fields, such as psychotherapy, counseling, science and research, business and education – particularly in adult education, teacher training and also school learning. ComTheo is a theological approach that is applied in various theological disciplines.

In this section, TCI and ComTheo can only be outlined. Ruth C. Cohn[2] and many other authors have described the concept of TCI. A description of TCI can be found in the *Handbook of Theme-Centered Interaction*.[3] H. Reiser comments critically on previous presentations of TCI, stating that TCI 'has its own pedagogical theory, which is, however, not articulated in the currently prevailing form of presentation.'[4] ComTheo has been presented and discussed in two book series[5] and numerous journal articles. Thus the aim of the following remarks is not to provide general descriptions of TCI and ComTheo, but rather to render the background comprehensible

---

    Innovative Modelle der Religionslehreraus- und -fortbildung. Bergisch Gladbach 2000, 55–68; Scharer Matthias, Lebendigen Lernprozessen trauen, Kompetenzen fördern. Das 'Innsbrucker Modell' der ReligionslehrerInnenausbildung unter der Herausforderung des Kompetenz- und Standarddiskurses in der Religionsdidaktik. In: *Österreichisches Religionspädagogisches Forum* (2013) 1, 58–63.

2   See, among others, Cohn and Farau, *Gelebte Geschichte der Psychotherapie.*

3   Schneider-Landolf, Mina, Spielmann, Jochen, and Zitterbarth, Walter (eds.), *Handbuch Themenzentrierte Interaktion (TZI)*, Göttingen 2009.

4   Reiser, Helmut (2014), Vorschlag für eine theoretische Grundlegung der Themenzentrierten Interaktion. In: *Themenzentrierte Interaktion. Theme-centered interaction* 2, 69–77, 69.

5   Hilberath, Bernd Jochen, and Scharer, Matthias (eds.), *Kommunikative Theologie.* Vols. 1–18. Mainz 2002–2005/Ostfildern 2006–2017; Hilberath, Bernd Jochen, Hinze, Bradford, and Scharer, Matthias (eds.), *Kommunikative Theologie – interdisziplinär/Communicative Theology – Interdisziplinary Studies.* Vols. 1–18. Münster 2004–2017. For the basic texts see, among others, Forschungskreis Kommunikative Theologie (ed.), *Kommunikative Theologie*; Scharer, Matthias, and Hilberath, Bernd Jochen (eds.), *The practice of Communicative Theology. Introduction to a new theological culture.* New York 2008; Hilberath, Bernd Jochen, and Scharer, Matthias, *Kommunikative Theologie. Grundlagen – Erfahrungen – Klärungen* (Kommunikative Theologie 15). Ostfildern 2013.

so that connections and continuations regarding interreligious religious pedagogy and religious didactics become transparent.

Theme-Centered Interaction and the Concept of Communicative Theology

To understand TCI and its importance for current educational policy, it is helpful to consider the life of its founder. Ruth C. Cohn linked her approach to a society-changing concern that is also relevant to our understanding of interreligious religious pedagogy and religious didactics.

Ruth C. Cohn and the 'Discovery' of TCI

As a German Jew, Ruth Charlotte[6] Cohn experienced the typical fate of a migrant: Born in Berlin in 1912 and raised in a liberal Jewish family, she and her Jewish friend and later husband were surprised by the nascent Nazi terror. Both emigrated in 1933, first to Switzerland, and then, in 1941, to the U.S. There, Cohn got divorced from her husband and lived as a single mother with two children in a faraway land and a foreign culture. Despite being well trained as a psychoanalyst, she did not receive a work permit. Nonetheless, she came into contact with education and learning. She developed the concept of TCI, which is also called 'Living Learning.' In the U.S., Cohn became one of the most important representatives of humanist psychology, collaborating closely with, among others, the founder of Gestalt Therapy, F. Perls, whose concept she criticized for its lack of world responsibility. In the 1970s, she returned to Europe, living initially in Switzerland. Later, when in need of care, she moved to Germany, where she died in 2010 at the age of 98.

Cohn's empathy for suffering and her fight against resignation played a significant role in the 'discovery' of TCI. She writes:

> I would like to encourage people, who do not want all this suffering, not to resign themselves to it and to feel faint, but instead to use their imagination and ability to

---

6 As a lifelong protest against Nazi rule, she shortened her German middle name Charlotte to C.

express themselves and to behave in solidarity, as long as we still feel autonomous forces in us. – That is the real thing that I would like with TCI.⁷

From the Individual to the Society

The challenging 'Globe' in which Ruth C. Cohn lived led her to extend her view from the subject orientation of psychoanalysis to a sociotherapeutic perspective, which she describes as follows: 'I experienced the horror of the time very deeply [...]. That I was able to live in Zurich seemed to me a strangely fateful gift.'⁸ For Cohn, the idea of the individual no longer living for himself or herself, but each in his or her social relatedness moved to the foreground after the experiences of the Holocaust and her survival: For the trained psychoanalyst, 'the couch was too small.'⁹

For her, education for all as living learning represented an effective way of changing society. Neither the authoritarian teaching style, which was was common in many schools and universities at the time, nor a laissez-faire teaching style, which was propagated in some American schools and found expression in the so-called anti-authoritarian pedagogy in Europe, were appropriate educational pathways for Cohn. For her, 'giving too little,' as she reproached the authoritarians for doing, was 'theft,' whereas 'giving too much,' as she learned from the advocates of a laissez-faire approach and anti-authoritarians, was, in her opinion, 'murder.'¹⁰ The right path lay between these two extremes, according to Cohn. In upbringing and education, it is important to acknowledge both one's authority and one's fallibility.¹¹

7   Cohn and Farau, *Gelebte Geschichte der Psychotherapie*, 374.
8   Ibid., 213.
9   Cohn, Ruth C., From Couch to circle to community. Beginnings of the Theme-Centered Interactional Method. In: Ruitenbeek, Hendrik Marinus (ed.), *Group Therapy Today*. New York 1969, 256–267.
10 Cohn, Ruth C., 'Zuwenig geben ist Diebstahl – zuviel geben ist Mord!' Gesprächspartner: Otto Herz (1981). In: Cohn, Ruth C., *Es geht ums Anteilnehmen... Perspektiven der Persönlichkeitsentfaltung in der Gesellschaft der Jahrtausendwende*. Freiburg i. Br. 1989, 142–152.
11 Cohn, Ruth C., 'Sich zur eigenen Autorität und Fehlbarkeit bekennen.' Gesprächspartner: Albert Biesinger and Thomas Schreijäck (1985). In: Cohn, *Es geht ums Anteilnehmen*, 127–141.

The Factors of 'Living' Teaching and Learning

In 1955, Ruth C. Cohn initiated a workshop on the subject of 'Counter-Transference.' According to her, in the psychotherapeutic setting, not only does the client transfer feelings onto the therapist, but also vice versa. Her way of working with the psychotherapists during this workshop became the starting point for TCI. In this context, she tells of a dream that gave her an intuitive insight into what made her teaching and guiding so vivacious. The dream had made TCI 'teachable,' according to her own statements:

> One night [...] I dreamed of an equilateral pyramid. When I woke up, I immediately realized that I had 'dreamed' the basis of my work. The equilateral dream pyramid meant to me: Four points define my group work. They are all four interconnected and equally important. These points are:
> - the person who turns to himself, the other and the theme (= Me);
> - the group members who become the group through mutual attention to the theme and interaction with the group (= We);
> - the theme, the task handled by the group (= It);
> - the environment that influences and is influenced by the group – thus, the environment in the nearest and broadest sense (= the Globe).[12]

The 'dream pyramid' became the famous equilateral triangle in the sphere, which has remained the symbol for TCI to this day.

The Ethos and the Attitude of Theme-Centered Interaction: Axioms and Postulates

TCI is based on a holistic image of the human being, recognizable in its axioms and postulates. The three TCI axioms, which we will explain in more detail below, communicate an idea of the good life for all humans, for all creatures, and ultimately for the entire cosmos. The two postulates represent the rules of the game in the application of the axioms of TCI.

---

12   Cohn and Farau, *Gelebte Geschichte der Psychotherapie*, 343f.

Ruth C. Cohn takes the psychosomatic wholeness of the human being as her starting point. She firmly resisted any attempt to reduce TCI to a method or technique for leading groups. She even changed the name of her approach from the original TIM (Theme-centered-Interactional Method) to TCI (English) and TZI (German).

From the point of view of TCI, a human being is a relationship-oriented being, a relational, communication-oriented subject that faces the challenge of combining autonomy and interdependence throughout its life in such a way that constructive development in oneself and with others becomes possible. Self-reliance and relatedness are intertwined dialectically: 'I am ever more autonomous, the more confidently I let the world into me.'[13] Increasing self-esteem results in increasing world consciousness and vice versa.

First Axiom

In the first axiom,[14] 'the dialectical oppositional integrity of autonomy and interdependence is converted through consciousness into a synthesis.'[15] The axiom relates to a thought process that takes into account opposites, ambivalences and paradoxes. By thematizing these, thus bringing them to mind and becoming amenable to decisions, they can lead to productive development.

From the dialectic of autonomy and interdependence, a specific cultural and social relationship emerges: The appropriation of the world takes place from early childhood onward in the tension between independence and personal responsibility and the reciprocal relatedness of people. Individual development occurs as one becomes increasingly conscious of the dialectic between autonomy and interdependence in one's own life context and confronts it.

---

13   Ibid., 357.
14   The first axiom states: 'The human is a psychological-biological unity and a part of the universe. He is therefore simultaneously autonomous and interdependent. The greater the autonomy of the individual, the more conscious he is of his interdependence with everyone' (ibid., 356).
15   Reiser, Helmut, Vorschlag für eine theoretische Grundlegung der Themenzentrierten Interaktion, 71.

The field of tension between the poles of self-determination or self-dependence and mutual dependence or influence is seen in TCI as a basic anthropological constant. Personal individual development always happens in relation to other people and in dealing with themes (tasks).[16]

A person becomes a complete human being when he or she confronts the world with its challenges, tasks and knowledge. Beyond the being-in-relationship of M. Buber, which is realized in the I-You-relationship, in TCI reference to the world is an equal and equivalent factor that belongs to being human.

Chairperson Postulate

Closely linked to the first axiom is the chairperson postulate,[17] the first of the two rules of TCI.[18] It does not simply dissolve the ambivalences in which people find themselves. Nor does it leave the human being incapable of acting. As a postulate, it encourages human development and action. One could perceive the first axiom together with the chairperson postulate as encouragement and empowerment to 'communicate alive in ambivalences.'[19]

The chairperson postulate makes it clear that for humans, in their multiple ambivalences, it is not simply about 'doing' something outwardly. The first step toward implementing the chairperson postulate is to look

---

16   Faßhauer, Uwe, 1. Axiom: existentiell-anthropologisches Axiom. In: Schneider-Landolf, Spielmann and Zitterbarth (eds.), *Handbuch Themenzentrierte Interaktion*, 80–85, 80.

17   The chairperson postulate, verbatim, states: 'Be your own chairman/your own chairwoman, be the chairperson of yourself. This means: – Be aware of your inner circumstances and your environment. – Take every situation as an offer for your decisions. Take and give, being responsible, as you want it to be for yourself and others' (Cohn and Farau, *Gelebte Geschichte der Psychotherapie*, 358).

18   It may seem strange that the first axiom is followed by the chairperson postulate. Nevertheless, there is an underlying conscious concept, whereby the TCI's 'rules of the game' are ideological axioms.

19   See the subtitle of the anthology of the 4th Congress of Communicative Theology, Juen, Maria, et al. (eds.), *Anders gemeinsam – gemeinsam anders? In Ambivalenzen lebendig kommunizieren* (Kommunikative Theologie, Vol. 18). Mainz 2015.

inward. It is necessary to perceive oneself as well as possible with all one's senses: 'Listen to your inner moods – your various needs, desires, motivations, ideas; use all of your senses – hear, see, smell, perceive!'[20] The gaze then turns outward:

> Use your mind, your knowledge, your judgment, your responsibility, your ability to think. Weighing decisions carefully. Nobody can take your decisions from you. You are the most important person in your world, as I am in mine. We need to be able to express ourselves clearly to one another and to listen carefully to each other, because this is our only bridge from island to island.[21]

The postulate protects against the paralyzing impotence that many people feel in the face of inscrutable economic and media contexts: 'I am not omnipotent; I am not impotent; I am partially powerful,'[22] as Cohn formulates it. In the face of violence and terror, however, we must acknowledge that we are not only partially powerful, but also partially powerless, and that we have to live with this partial powerlessness. The chairperson principle is misunderstood if it is interpreted as an invitation to a self-actualization that does not involve relatedness.

Second Axiom

The second axiom, or the ethical axiom,[23] refers to the difficult question of what is humane and therefore worthy of protection. Cohn does not give a theoretical answer, but rather offers concrete examples:

> Being humane, for example, means not tormenting living things and killing any more of them than is necessary to sustain and promote one's life (especially human beings); the term killing also includes the killing of mental and spiritual capacities.[24]

---

20 Cohn, Ruth C., *Von der Psychoanalyse zur themenzentrierten Interaktion. Von der Behandlung einzelner zu einer Pädagogik für alle*. Stuttgart 2009, 164.
21 Ibid.
22 Cohn and Farau, *Gelebte Geschichte der Psychotherapie*, 359.
23 The second axiom reads: 'Awe is due to all that is alive and to its growth. Respect for growth conditionally evaluative decisions. The humane is valuable, inhumaneness is threatening value' (ibid., 357).
24 Ibid.

According to Matzdorf and Cohn, one can see the humane in a person's loving, knowing and acting behavior. The inhumane is evident in 'sinful' and 'careless' behavior. In this context, Cohn deals with the question of whether there is absolute good and evil, which have been established for humankind, and how these relate to the cognitive and decision-making abilities of humankind. Cohn opposes the idea of absolute good and evil, but she believes that ethical works are 'indispensable' and 'process-dependent':

> I can only speak my truth and not yours. But I believe that differing aspects of the ethos could not exist if they did not refer to the reality of an essential center.[25]

Thus, she holds the hypothesis of an inherent 'organismic' sense of value. Cohn considers its unfolding to be a question of survival for humanity which corresponds to man as an autonomous interdependent subject.

Third Axiom

In addition to the ethical axiom, another axiom supports the co-evolution of humankind toward self-direction through autonomy and interdependence. This third axiom is the so-called pragmatic-political axiom.[26] According to this axiom, human beings have the necessary freedom to make decisions about and to independently structure their lives. Thus, it is essential that the limits are variable. Human beings act responsibly by using the inner and outer space of freedom, when they know about the universal conditionality of freedom. Value consciousness and the capacity to act and be responsible, which is strengthened by the attitude and method of TCI, are supposed to prevent human

---

25 Ibid., 467.
26 The third axiom reads: 'Free decision happens within conditional inner and outer limits, extension of these limits is possible. Execution: Our degree of freedom, when we are healthy, intelligent, materially secure, and spiritually mature, is greater than when we are sick, limited or poor and suffer from violence and lack of maturity' (ibid., 357).

catastrophes, like those experienced by Ruth C. Cohn on the run from the Holocaust.

Compared to a fatalistic existentialism, which originated in Europe, Cohn represents an existentialism that strengthens the individual as a subject and not only grants him conditional possibilities for freedom and decision-making, but actively promotes them. The question of whether a direct or indirect obligation to political action can be deduced from the pragmatic political axiom is a controversial subject of discussion in TCI.[27]

Disturbance Postulate

TCI was and is reproached – often from among its own ranks – for being idealistic and harmonizing. As a trained psychoanalyst, Cohn knew that the experience of resistance offers learning opportunities for humankind. Out of this awareness she formulated the so-called disturbance postulate. The original English formulation, 'Disturbances and passionate involvements take precedence,'[28] does not have the negative character of 'disturbances,' which are considered as behavioral and learning disorders in school contexts that stop the learning process, and thus are inappropriate and irritating.

When disturbances and passionate involvements remain unspoken or suppressed in the long term, 'impersonal, "trouble-free" classrooms, lecture

27 A number of authors (Günther Hoppe, Helmut Johach, Manfred Krämer, Gernot Klemmer, and others) believe or believed that the political momentum of TCI is currently underdeveloped or no longer in keeping with the heritage of Ruth C. Cohn. They called for stronger social and political awareness in TCI. This demand is often associated with criticism of Globe oblivion. The controversy over the socio-critical and political claim of TCI also relates to the question of where political action begins. Is the empowerment of the chairperson already political, or does TCI-compliant learning mean to intervene in the socio-political discourse and actively change inhumane structures?

28 Kroeger, Matthias, Das sogenannte Störungspostulat: 'Disturbances and passionate involvements take precedence.' In: von Kanitz, Anja, et al., *Elemente der Themenzentrierten Interaktion. Texte zur Aus- und Weiterbildung.* Göttingen 2015, 132–144, 132.

halls, factory rooms, and meeting rooms'[29] come into being. The political and societal significance of the disturbance postulate became apparent early on. For A. Ockel and R. Cohn, many people are subject to 'disturbance' due to the fact 'that we overlook all that is humanly possible, because we are paralyzed by the humanly impossible.'[30] As if written in response to the helplessness of Europe vis-à-vis the challenge of large refugee flows, in 1992 both authors mention the following aspect as the most important 'generative theme':

> What do I do, as a single person or as a small group in the face of unmanageable factors that appear to be needed to solve political and social problems?[31]

Compass and Operating Principle of TCI

In Ruth C. Cohn's dream, the TCI factors I, WE, IT and GLOBE were introduced and named according to her early intuition. Their interconnection is shown in Figure 1.

The equilateral triangle with the TCI factors at the respective corners and the sphere or circle as the GLOBE, which affects each of the other factors, is not a static symbol, but rather signals the living, dynamic balance of the system: The TCI factors come into play again and again, new and different, depending on where the respective learning group is currently moving. If it is heavily involved in the IT, that is, in the matter or the tasks, then attention is focused on the individual, the group or class, or on the context in which one is learning to regain balance.

---

29   Cohn and Farau, *Gelebte Geschichte der Psychotherapie*, 357.
30   Ockel, Anita, and Cohn, Ruth C., Das Konzept des Widerstands in der Themenzentrierten Interaktion. Vom psychoanalytischen Konzept des Widerstands über das TZI-Konzept der Störung zum Ansatz der Gesellschaftstherapie. In: Löhmer, Cornelia, and Standhardt, Rüdiger (eds.), *TZI. Pädagogisch-therapeutische Gruppenarbeit nach Ruth C. Cohn*. Stuttgart ²1993, 177–206, 202.
31   Ibid.

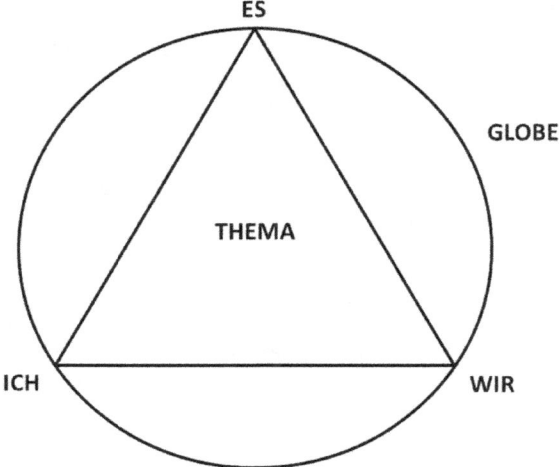

Figure 1. 'Dream pyramid' of Theme-Centered Interaction

The German expressions in the graphic correspond to the following English terms: ES [IT], GLOBE [GLOBE], WIR [WE], ICH [I], and THEMA [THEME].

Consideration of the TCI factors and the dynamic balance is not only important as a compass for a living learning process; it also helps in the planning of teaching and learning processes and provides guidelines for a comprehensive evaluation. The realization of the apparently simple TCI work tool requires, in practice, a lot of attention to the concrete participants in the learning process, the dynamics that develop between them, the existential depth dimension of the concerns, and the GLOBE, or the context of college, school and instruction. All four factors are equivalent in TCI, such that both the rigidity of the material in the learning event and its slippage in 'soul striptease,' group dynamics or contextual editing are permanently avoided.

Every meaningful teaching and learning process touches on objects, matters or contents that are involved in teaching and learning. These do not always have to be verbalized. Nonverbal representations, such as symbolic objects and symbolic actions (e.g. rites and gestures) play a major role in (inter-)religious learning. Ruth C. Cohn speaks of the IT when it comes to the 'thing.' Teachers know that the subject matter or content that is communicated during learning is more than a neutral thing or content in an abstract sense. Even a seemingly objective text is – as soon as it is communicated – already colored by the interests, ideas, emotions, resistances, etc., of the speaker, the social affinity of the group in which it is communicated, and the respective contextual conditions, which influence the learning process. This is not only the case in school, but also in a scientific context.[32]

Especially in religious learning, the I of the individual pupil or the WE of a group or class or the context (GLOBE) can become the current subject of learning. Thus, it is also meaningful to distinguish between the object or content that is being taught or learned and the theme, which is very specific and which stimulates learning. Consequently, in TCI, a differentiation between the subject of learning (content, concerns), that is, the IT, and the respective theme, has become commonplace. Therefore, the theme is no longer located close to the IT in Figure 1, but forms the center of the triangle in the sphere.[33] Thus, the theme can refer to the IT, the I, the WE or the GLOBE.

The centering of the theme in the middle of the triangle in the sphere also implies that the structure of the learning processes, which is determined by forms of work, methods and media, is a direct result of the theme. Teachers, in particular, often spend a lot of time and energy finding the right forms of work, methods and media. The question of how a learning process can be structured is generally easier and faster if the theme has been clarified as well as possible beforehand. This also applies to the concrete formulation of the theme, which is the subject of special attention in TCI. As we already mentioned, special attention is paid to the language play of creative theme formulations in lesson planning and TCI learning. Appropriate and creative theme formulations and their effects are practiced and tested in TCI training and should be part of any teacher training.

The theme is seen as the specific management tool in TCI learning processes. The deliberately formulated and personally introduced TCI theme differs from the theme concept common in didactics. The latter usually refers to the content or tasks as the theme. Often no learning-generating or communication-controlling importance is attached to the linguistic form

---

32 See Habermas, Jürgen, *Erkenntnis und Interesse. Mit einem neuen Nachwort.* Frankfurt a. M. 2001.
33 See, among others, Langmaack, Barbara, *Einführung in die Themenzentrierte Interaktion TZI. Leben rund ums Dreieck.* Weinheim 2001.

of the theme. Furthermore, the role that those involved in the learning process play in finding and formulating the theme is usually overlooked. Cohn reports that it was only through listening attentively to people's personal narratives that the concrete theme took on a distinctive shape: 'I spoke to them as a co-seeker, helping them to find their generative themes.'[34] The notion of 'generative themes' points to the relationship of TCI, especially its understanding of the theme, with the liberation pedagogical work of Paulo Freire.[35] The theme-centered attention in the learning process makes it possible to spontaneously grasp that which is central and existentially significant and to bring it into play, including through metaphors, among other things. At the same time, subject sensitivity can expose inconsequential discussions as such. The ability to redesign a learning process (including student participation) because the originally introduced theme has changed or petered out represents a special theme competence.

Early Receptions of TCI in the Theological Church Context

As a psychoanalyst and group therapist, Ruth C. Cohn had largely avoided religious questions during her years in the U.S., so it is all the more astonishing that TCI quickly found favor with churches and theology after her return to Europe. It should be kept in mind that Protestant church historian Matthias Kroeger from Hamburg, whose *Theme-Centered Pastoral Care*[36] was the first German-language book on TCI, contributed a great deal to the dissemination of TCI within Christian churches, especially Protestant churches, and more widely. Josef Mayer-Scheu's implementation of TCI in the church context also

---

34   Cohn and Farau, *Gelebte Geschichte der Psychotherapie*, 334.
35   See Hagleitner, Silvia, *Mit Lust an der Welt – in Sorge um sie. Feministisch-politische Bildungsarbeit nach Paulo Freire und Ruth C. Cohn*. Mainz 1996; Ostertag, Margit, Von Ruth Cohn und Paulo Freire lernen. Annäherungen an eine bildungstheoretisch fundierte Hochschuldidaktik. In: Miller, Tilly, and Ostertag, Margit (eds.), *Hochschulbildung. Wiederaneignung eines existentiell bedeutsamen Begriffs*. Berlin 2017, 123–133.
36   Kroeger, Matthias, *Themenzentrierte Seelsorge. Über die Kombination klientenzentrierter und themenzentrierter Arbeit nach Carl R. Rogers und Ruth C. Cohn in Theologie und schulischer Gruppenarbeit*. Stuttgart 1989.

exerted a great influence, especially on hospital pastoral care. The well-known practical theologian of the Protestant Faculty at the University of Marburg, Dietrich Stollberg, made TCI theoretically and practically known at the university and beyond.[37]

An article entitled 'TCI in church practice,'[38] published in 1992, focused on the many examples of the use of TCI in pastoral care, religious education and church community work. Bernhard Honsel's community model was particularly impressive and well known in pastoral theology. Honsel attempted to lead a Catholic community to TCI and had TCI graduates working in his team.[39] Michael Frickel developed the model of theme-centered meditation.[40] Helga Modesto traveled throughout Latin America and Siberia with her husband Pietro and introduced TCI to many church communities including a large number of bishops and others of high rank in the religious orders.

Since the early 1970s, theologians have been attempting to implement the values and attitudes of TCI and its methodology in pastoral, further educational and religious pedagogical training and practice. At the Ruth Cohn Institute International, the ecumenical group 'TCI and Theology' was formed in the earliest days of the institute.[41]

Due to the widespread use of TCI in the Christian churches, there was an increasing need for a theological foundation for TCI and greater penetration. On this subject, Dieter Funke described, in his work on *Verkündung zwischen Tradition and Interaction*,[42] the TCI Group as an open social situation in which 'thematic-symbolic orientation' could happen. This orientation was seen 'as a qualitative change in everyday consciousness by

---

[37] See, among others, Stollberg, Dietrich, *Lernen, weil es Freude macht. Eine Einführung in die Themenzentrierte Interaktion*. Munich 1982.

[38] Scharer, Matthias, TZI in der kirchlichen Praxis. In: Löhmer and Standhardt (eds.), *TZI*, 312–325.

[39] See Honsel, Bernhard, *Der rote Punkt. Eine Gemeinde unterwegs*. Düsseldorf 1985.

[40] See, among others, Frickel, Michael, Von der TZI zur themenzentrierte Meditation. Grund und Ziel einer Änderung. In: Löhmer and Standhardt (eds.), *TZI*, 218–229.

[41] See <http://www.tzi-theologie.net> [accessed on February 10, 2017].

[42] Funke, Dieter, *Verkündigung zwischen Tradition und Interaktion. Praktisch-theologische Studien zur Themenzentrierten Interaktion (TZI) nach Ruth C. Cohn*. Frankfurt a. M. 1984.

addressing the symbols of Christianity.'[43] This theological reconstruction of TCI constituted important preparatory work for a theological reception of TCI as it had been developed in Communicative Theology. In the program of Communicative Theology[44] (hereafter referred to as ComTheo), a new theological reception of TCI is used, which should be understood more as a style of theologizing than as a rigid model and should be – despite the initial inner Christian situation – open and accommodating in relation to other religious traditions.

The Approach of Communicative Theology (ComTheo)

Communicative Theology was developed with the intention of connecting theology with practice. Matthias Scharer and Bernd Jochen Hilberath began to generate and develop theological issues from a systematic-theological and practical-theological perspective together with practitioners in theological training courses. TCI represented an important approach in terms of a methodology.

The aim of the university program Communicative Theology was to make theology tangible and to 'get into the belly' – into one's own life – to be able to 'incorporate' it, so to speak.

An essential feature of the reception of TCI in ComTheo is that it is no longer a matter of *applying* TCI in church practice or using it to enliven theology. Rather, the instrument of TCI, the triangle in the sphere, is becoming an *orientation instrument* for theological teaching and research. Even the axioms and postulates of TCI are understood theologically in ComTheo and further developed and expanded as specific options (in the theological sense).[45]

---

43   Ibid., 200–343.
44   In this context, the dissertation of the systematic theologian Gunda Werner, which was published much later, has to be mentioned as it also adopted TCI from a theological perspective: Werner, Gunda, *Macht Glaube glücklich? Freiheit und Bezogenheit als Erfahrung persönlicher Heilszusage*. Regensburg 2005.
45   Forschungskreis Kommunikative Theologie (ed.), *Kommunikative Theologie*, 18–23.

Levels and Dimensions of Communicative Theology

The research and teaching style of Communicative Theology unfolds in a networking process of different dimensions (one's own life and faith experience, community experience, context or globe experience and biblical witnesses in living mediation or religious-ideological traditions) and – that is, alongside theological orientation, one of its most striking differences to TCI – different levels (immediate level of participation, level of experience and interpretation, level of scientific reflection). In the following presentation of ComTheo, we begin with the immediate level of participation.

The Immediate Participation Level in its Dimensions

A special feature of ComTheo is that theological research and teaching tackles current and living interaction and communication. As in TCI, it is, first of all, the individual persons (TCI: I) who do something with themselves in these processes and thereby become affected or involved. However, this does not happen independently, but rather in interaction and communication with others. This creates the different social constitutions (the different WEs) in which the individuals are involved.

From a scientific perspective, the I–WE relationship and the training of a WE that is capable of communicating and working is a complex process, which should be religious pedagogically and religious didactically reflected and competently supervised.

Interacting and communicating is not an end in itself, but rather always involves an object of communication, a 'what is at stake,' a topic or – in other words – a factual point of view (TCI speaks of IT). Here, the I–WE–IT communication, as we have already seen in the section on TCI, takes place in a concrete societal, political, economic, historical and cultural context (TCI: GLOBE).[46]

What is significant is that the relationship between the individual dimensions has a passive and an active aspect: The GLOBE affects people, communities, and issues, and, conversely, people, groups, and issues have

---

46 See ibid., 70–74.

an impact on and change the GLOBE. This interaction also affects the other dimensions. Thus, the dynamics of communities (groups) affect individuals and vice versa.

The Experience and Interpretation Levels and their Dimensions

Based on our experience, the process does not stop. Humans possess the ability to symbolically represent experience. This ability to symbolize (be it by means of language, signs or symbols in a narrower sense) brings with it the possibility of dissociation, reflection and experience formation, and thereby enables references regardless of the current state of experience. Also on the level of experience and interpretation, the gaze of ComTheo enters four dimensions, in which reflected and symbolically processed experience formation takes place: The dimension of one's own individual life and faith experience, which includes subjective experience formations, interpretations, concepts and constructions (I-experience); the communal experience dimension or – interpreted in Christian terms – church community belonging (WE-experience), which brings into focus the dynamics of the intersubjective and the communicative; the dimension of the religious tradition formation (Christian: biblical testimonials in living mediation and other religious traditions), which constitutes the third dimension of experience and interpretation (IT-experience); and the GLOBE, or the context, in the sense of the formation of experience and interpretation, represented as 'text,' which must be 'read' and interpreted anew in each case.

The Scientific Reflection Level and its Dimensions

Scientific activity is characterized by comprehensibility and methodical procedure. As a scientific program, Communicative Theology cannot stop at the level of experience and interpretation; instead, it develops another level, the level of scientific reflection. This level aims to methodically guide and link together the immediate level of participation and the level of experience and interpretation with the individual dimensions. Thus,

ComTheo speaks of the biographical dimension (I), the intersubjective-communicative dimension (WE), the globe dimension (GLOBE) and the dimension of scientific-theological sources – theories that are based on living traditions (IT).[47] On the scientific level of reflection, the individual dimensions – changing across all other levels and dimensions – become locations of scientific-theological knowledge.[48] So, for example, in the biographic-scientific dimension, starting from living current processes in which the I is involved as I, through the reflected and interpreted biographical life and faith experience to biography, as a scientific-theological cognitive form, links are made under biographical focus and theological findings are gained. A similar approach is applied to the other sites of knowledge. Each location of knowledge or each dimension (biography, interaction/community experience, reflected traditions in the sense of theories, models, methodologies as a source of scientific knowledge, GLOBE) is multi-linked, on the one hand, with the same dimensions of other levels and, on the other, with different dimensions on the same level. At the same time, these locations have different scientific tasks: They are sources of perception, sources of cognition, and – as far as the implementation aspect is concerned – sources of theological-scientific testimony.

In scientific teaching and research, not all of the dimensions are always illuminated in the same way. The different theological approaches also take a closer look at different dimensions, such as, for example, biographical theology or contextual theology, and so on and so forth. In contrast, the approach of ComTheo seeks to make it clear that in a conceptually reflected understanding of high-quality theology, all dimensions must be reflected on.

The current context has shown that it is necessary to open up the religious approach and worldview of ComTheo and thus make it accessible

---

47   Kraml, Martina, The published word is not the final one … Kontingenzsensible theologische Forschung auf dem Hintergrund des Forschungsprogrammes Kommunikative Theologie. In: *Zeitschrift für katholische Theologie* (2014) 136, 233-250.
48   See, from a Christian perspective, the loci-theologici-teaching and here, for example, Seckler, Max, *Die schiefen Wände des Lehrhauses*. Freiburg i. Br. 1988.

to the perspectives of people of other religions and worldviews. The establishment of a degree program in Islamic Religious Pedagogy has given rise to the possibility of doing this.

Attitudes and Options

The crucial methodological feature of ComTheo lies not only in the networking of dimensions and levels. This would be too mechanical and methodical. In the concept of ComTheo, as in TCI, the way of communicating and theologizing represents a constitutive feature of the knowledge-generating methodology: People's attitudes and approaches manifest themselves best in decision-making situations, because the direction of their decisions become clear in such situations. In Christian, primarily Protestant and Catholic, theology, one hears discussion of 'options.' ComTheo has agreed upon seven options that are indispensable to its theological activity. The first three options stem from TCI and were further interpreted theologically; the others were developed from a specifically Christian perspective.[49]

The Understanding of Communication of ComTheo

Out of theological interest, ComTheo uses the term 'communication' and not the term 'interaction' or the like. It differentiates between these against the background of concerns of TCI and the Christian theological traditions, thus distancing ComTheo from a technical understanding.

ComTheo does not simply accept the Jürgen Habermas' theory of communicative action, which flowed into Christian theology through

---

49   The theologically interpreted axioms of the TCI are: Man in relationship – disposed and free; Creation and incarnation establish awe and respect; Limitation and extension of boundaries in the face of God's universal will to salvation. The other options of communicative theology gained from theology are: Option for serenity by grace in the face of all feasibility fantasies; Option for the poor; Option for 'staying in,' even if nothing works; Option for the Contemplatio and Mystic-Mystagogical. See, in this regard: Forschungskreis Kommunikative Theologie (ed.), *Kommunikative Theologie*, 94.

Helmut Peukert and Edmund Arens.[50] The concept of understanding in ComTheo, which has its origins in the anthropological understandings of Ruth C. Cohn, Martin Buber, Emanuel Lévinas, Paul Ricœur[51] and others, leads toward a theological,[52] relationship- and encounter-oriented understanding of communication that eludes technical producibility. Since ComTheo is specifically related to the Christian understanding of communication from a theological perspective, it ties in with the self-communication of God in the cosmos and the history of salvation, but especially the history of God with the people in the destiny of Jesus Christ.[53] In this way, a person, rather than content, is the focus of the theologically understood communication event. The spiritual gift of each person enables a living mediation of the revelation. The current historical and cultural situation and all human beings are included and suspended in it – notwithstanding the ambivalences, destructive mechanisms and violent phenomena that shape them.[54]

The Engagement of ComTheo in Interreligious Communication

After a congress in Innsbruck in 2003, which was dedicated to the inner Christian theme of the Trinity, and another in 2005 in Tübingen, at which Christian ecumenism was discussed, in 2008 Communicative Theology dared to take an exceptional step: A 'Twin-Congress' was held in New York and Telfs, dedicated, on the one hand, to the internal cultural diversity of the church in America, and focused, on the other hand – in Telfs – on the encounter between Muslims and Christians.[55] One of the sources for the work at the congress was empirical research that had been conducted in advance of the big event in the form of a separate conference

---

50   See Aren, Edmund, *Gottesverständigung: Eine kommunikative Religionstheologie*. Freiburg i. Br. 2007.
51   See Hilberath and Scharer, *Kommunikative Theologie*, 122–139.
52   Forschungskreis Kommunikative Theologie (ed.), *Kommunikative Theologie*, 45f.
53   See ibid., 52.
54   See ibid.
55   See Kästle, Kraml and Mohagheghi (eds.), *Heilig-Tabu*.

in Telfs.[56] Thus, the authentic testimonies of Muslims, Christians and people without any explicit commitment could flow into the congress. In 2013, a revised edition[57] of the basic volume *Communicative Theology* was published by Bernd Jochen Hilberath and Matthias Scharer. In 2014, the 4th Congress on Communicative Theology, titled 'Different Together – Together Different. Communicating Alive in the Ambivalences of the Present,'[58] took place.

In 2008, Muslim–Catholic collaboration began. One result of this collaboration was the introduction of the bachelor's program in Islamic Religious Education in the School of Education at the University of Innsbruck. This collaboration gave rise to the possibility of realizing the desire to open up Communicative Theology and the Innsbruck model of religious didactics and, on that basis, develop new perspectives appropriate to an interreligious religious pedagogy and religious didactics.

Muslim History and Access to the 'Innsbruck Model'

History of Religious Education in Islam

If one considers the genesis of religions, one can hardly ignore the fact that every religion is primarily about the upbringing or education of humankind. Religions are thus all aimed at educational processes that focus on the initiation and support of the 'the process of becoming human.' In this context, Islam should also be seen as an Islamic way of becoming human.

Islam also attaches particular importance to the education of the human being. This strong educational character is evident in the primary source of Islam, the Qur'an, as well as the tradition of the Prophet (*Sunnah*), the second most important Islamic source. The first verses that were revealed to Muhammad (Sura 96:1–5) can be interpreted, according to Muslim

---

[56] See Panhofer, Johannes, Eintauchen in die 'interreligiöse Lebenswelt.' Methodisch geleitete Erkundungen im Dialogprozess der Jännertagung. In: Kästle, Kraml and Mohagheghi (eds.), *Heilig-Tabu*, 107–119.
[57] Hilberath and Scharer, *Kommunikative Theologie*.
[58] Kästle, Kraml and Mohagheghi (eds.), *Heilig-Tabu*.

scholars, as a call to education. This underscores the importance of education and knowledge acquisition through revelation itself.

In addition to this general call for education, there are numerous other Qur'an verses that highlight the human ability to educate and the human need to be educated.[59] The *Sunnah* takes the same position as the Qur'an on this point. Numerous statements by the Prophet on the subjects of education and knowledge acquisition testify to a particularly positive approach to education.[60] Sebastian Günther stresses this aspect of Islam:

> In the Qur'an [...] one repeatedly finds concrete statements both on the transmission and on the appropriation of religious and profane knowledge and on cognitive understanding.[61]

The fundamentally positive attitude of the Qur'an and the Prophetic Tradition toward education has, from the very beginning, led Muslims to engage intensively with the question of the nature of Islamic education. It should be noted that in the early Islamic period there was no explicit distinction between general education and religious education. Education was understood more as an overall process, which, in spite of the possible differences in the subject matter, was always oriented toward God. This holistic approach to human education resulted in Islamic society flourishing between the ninth and thirteenth centuries, spurred on by its own papermaking, and evolving into a 'knowledge society.'[62]

In addition to Islam's appreciative attitude toward education in general and religious education in particular, there were practical reasons that led Muslims to think about an appropriate means of transmitting their religion early on: The rapid expansion of Islamic law and the rapid increase

---

59   See Qur'an 4:28, 2:31.
60   See Günther, Sebastian, Bildungsauffassungen klassischer muslimischer Gelehrter. Von Abu Hanifa bis Ibn Khaldun (8.–15. Jh.). In: Sejdini (ed.), *Islamische Theologie und Religionspädagogik in Bewegung*, 51–71, 53.
61   Günther, Sebastian, Das Buch ist ein Gefäß gefüllt mit Wissen und Scharfsinn. In: Gemeinhardt, Peter, and Günther, Sebastian (eds.), *Von Rom nach Bagdad. Bildung und Religion von der römischen Kaiserzeit bis zum klassischen Islam*. Tübingen 2013, 357–379, 358.
62   Günther, Bildungsauffassungen klassischer muslimischer Gelehrter, 53.

in the number of new Muslims meant that such a means of transmitting their religion was indispensable for the fulfillment of the Islamic educational mission and for the consolidation of the new community. The new Muslims were to be entrusted with the Qur'an and the teachings of Islam as quickly as possible, so that they could shape their lives and live accordingly and share this new way of life with other people. Moreover, it must be remembered that initially the 'students' were adults who came from different socio-cultural contexts and therefore had to be taught differently.

When asked how religious education should be shaped, the focus was first on the actions of the Prophet, who is considered by Muslims to be the first human teacher and whose religious actions were under divine supervision. To this day, the actions and attitudes of the Prophet in the promulgation of the religious message are not infrequently considered to be a model for contemporary religious education. The Prophet's function as an example is grounded in the special position that is attributed to him in the Qur'an, among other things. Thus, for example, Sura 33, verse 21 states:

> VERILY, in the Apostle of God, you have a good example for everyone who looks forward [with hope and awe] to God and the Last Day and remembers God unceasingly.[63]

Initially, Islamic education took place in private homes. Since the new Muslim community in Mecca was oppressed and harassed, it had to gather in private homes to pray together and be educated in religious matters. Only after the emigration to Medina (AD 622), where the Muslims were welcomed and where they established themselves as a constitutive part of the society, did they build their prayer houses, which from then on were also centers of religious education. The Prophet himself had attached great importance to the construction of the first mosque in Medina. A space for the teaching and learning of religion was established within the mosque building.

Mosques remained for a long time the centers of religious education. Scholars, along with their followers or students, formed a circle of knowledge within the mosque and, in this way, passed on religious knowledge from various fields. As the number of Muslims began to grow, it became

---

63   Asad, *The Message of the Qur'an*, 721.

necessary to found new institutions exclusively dedicated to religious education. The most famous and long-lasting educational institution of this kind was the *madrasa*.[64] This word means 'the place where teaching occurs' and it was used as an umbrella term for various types of educational institutions.[65]

In addition to teaching, Muslim scholars composed various writings and were thus able to express their opinions on general and religious education. It should be noted that the medieval scholars who dealt with the subject of education were active in various areas of Islamic sciences. Their writings did not include a theory of education, but instead focused on concrete advice for the design of the lesson and the correct behavior of teachers and students. Among the most important scholars who composed writings on the subject of Islamic education are, inter alia, Ibn Sahnun (d. 854) and Jahiz (d. 868), but also Muslim philosophers such as Ibn Sina (d. 1037), Ibn Rushd (d. 1198), and the mystic Ghazali (d. 1111).

Sebastian Günther aptly describes the religious educational achievements of Muslim scholars based on their writings in the following terms:

> These writings also testify to the wealth of ideas and creativity of their authors, as well as to open-mindedness of medieval Muslims to study educational philosophical designs from earlier periods of human history and non-Islamic cultures and, as long as these were consistent with the religious principles of the Qur'an, to render them usable for the well-being of the community.[66]

After the collapse of the Ottoman Empire at the beginning of the twentieth century, individual Muslim states or regions pursued their own paths in the field of religious education, determined by their contexts, so that henceforth one could no longer speak of an Islamic religious pedagogy in a comprehensive and uniform sense.

---

64   See Bozkurt, Nebi, Medrese. In: Türkiye Diyanet vakfı (ed.), *İslâm ansiklopedisi. Standardausgabe*. İstanbul 1988, 323–327.
65   See Schoeler, Gregor, Gesprochenes Wort und Schrift. Mündlichkeit und Schriftlichkeit im frühislamischen Lehrbetrieb. In: Gemeinhardt and Günther (eds.), *Von Rom nach Bagdad*, 269–289.
66   Günther, Das Buch ist ein Gefäß gefüllt mit Wissen und Scharfsinn, 364.

Approaches in the European Context

In contrast to countries with majority Muslim populations, the history of Islamic religious pedagogy in Western Europe is relatively young and closely linked to the immigration of Muslim workers in the 1960s and 1970s. As in the time of the founding of Islam, mosques and prayer houses in Western Europe were and still are centers of religious education for Muslims. Since religious education took place mainly in mosques, it was shaped by an understanding that Muslims had brought from their home countries. Considering that the imams, who were responsible for spiritual direction and mosque teaching, were trained almost exclusively in other contexts, and, for the most part, knew neither the culture nor the language of the country in which they were living and working for a few years, it is not surprising that none of the approaches developed in the field of Islamic religious education could be applied in the present European context.

But this was not the only reason why Muslims in Europe had to content themselves for decades with theological and religious pedagogical approaches from their countries of origin. The theological and religious pedagogical dependence of these Muslims, who have been living in Western Europe for 50 years, has been promoted by the enduring lack of interest of politics, society, educational institutions and Muslim associations in a theological or religious pedagogical integration of Islam into the European context. The mosques could not accomplish this integration and spiritual belongingness, for understandable reasons, since they were formed on the basis of ethnic groups and were run by imams who had been trained abroad. A new place had to be found where Muslims could reflect anew on their religion in the European context.

It took a long time for those in charge to recognize the need for a theological or religious pedagogical integration of Muslims into Europe, which would make complete integration possible and counteract radical tendencies, of which many Muslim youths are helplessly at the mercy. Gradually, Islamic centers developed at German-speaking universities. These were supposed to rethink Islamic theology and religious pedagogy from a European perspective and develop new approaches. In this context, the German Science Council, which recommended the introduction of Islamic theological studies at German universities in its 2010 report, expects from the newly founded Islamic Theological Studies 'Islamic Norms and Values – parallel to the positions and perspectives of other religions – to be properly reflected in academic as well as public debates.'[67]

However, the establishment of Islamic centers for theological and religious pedagogical studies at German-speaking universities is only the first step toward the development of new theological and religious pedagogical approaches in the European context. These first steps must be followed by more concrete research, on the basis of which the foundations of contextual approaches, which correspond to the reality of Muslims living in Europe, can be developed.

Currently, Islamic religious pedagogy in the European context is also in the making. Initial approaches are emerging that differ from location to location and from person to person. There is, however, consensus that no well-developed concepts in Islamic religious pedagogy are currently available.[68] This is understandable insofar as Islamic theology and religious pedagogy is still new to German-speaking universities and therefore 'the scientific debate in the area of theological-religious pedagogy [...] is currently still in a phase of orientation and self-ascertainment.'[69]

---

67   Wissenschaftsrat, Empfehlungen zur Weiterentwicklung von Theologien und religionsbezogenen Wissenschaften an deutschen Hochschulen. Internet resource: <http://www.wissenschaftsrat.de/download/archiv/9678-10.pdf> [accessed on February 15, 2017], 76.

68   See Ucar, Bülent, Synopse für das Fach 'Islamunterricht' in der Grundschule: Zwischen didaktischem Profil und inhaltlicher Gestaltung. In: Kiefer, Michael, Gottwald, Eckart, and Ucar, Bülent (eds.), *Auf dem Weg zum islamischen Religionsunterricht. Sachstand und Perspektiven in Nordrhein-Westfalen*. Berlin 2008, 121–140, 121; Bilgin, Beyza, *Egitim Bilimi ve Din Egitimi*. Ankara 1988, 4; Aslan, Ednan, 'Wir erwarten europaweit Impulse'. Die Stimme eines Hochschullehrers. In: Behr, Harry Harun, Rohe, Mathias, and Schmid, Hansjörg (eds.), *'Den Koran zu lesen genügt nicht!'. Fachliches Profil und realer Kontext für ein neues Berufsfeld. Auf dem Weg zum Islamischen Religionsunterricht*. Berlin 2008, 63–74.

69   Sejdini, Zekirija, Grundlagen eines theologiesensiblen und beteiligtenbezogenen Modells islamischer Religionspädagogik und Religionsdidaktik im deutschsprachigen Kontext. In: *Österreichisches Religionspädagogisches Forum* (2015) 1, 21–28, 22.

Even if there are as yet hardly any comprehensive concepts in Islamic religious pedagogy and religious didactics, there are, in the German-speaking realm, some new, authentic approaches, which, despite different emphases, have a high compatibility with the general religious pedagogical and religious didactic discourse.[70]

Muslim Access to the 'Innsbruck Model of Religious Didactics'

In the self-discovery process of Islamic religious pedagogy and religious didactics, the close collaboration between the faculties of Catholic and Islamic religious pedagogy has led to an intensive examination of the 'Innsbruck model of religious didactics.' In this context, from a Muslim perspective, the legitimate question arises of why a religious pedagogical or religious didactic concept that has originated in a Christian context can be the basis for an interreligious religious pedagogy. To what extent can this model correspond to or fulfill the ideas of Islamic religious pedagogy and religious didactics? These questions arise, in particular, when one assumes that both religions must have completely different religious pedagogical approaches, since they were not only created and developed in different contexts, but also differ in their 'essence.' Here, it becomes clear that the notion of religion, theology and religious pedagogy significantly determines the attitude to our approach. This issue will be briefly taken up in the next section.

[70] See Behr, Harry Harun, *Islamische Bildungslehre*. Garching 1998; Behr, Harry Harun, Bildungstheoretisches Nachdenken als Grundlage für eine islamische Religionsdidaktik. In: Kaddor, Lamya (ed.), *Islamische Erziehungs- und Bildungslehre*. Berlin 2008, 49–65; Sejdini, Zwischen Gewissheit und Kontingenz; Sejdini (ed.), *Islamische Theologie und Religionspädagogik in Bewegung*; Sarikaya, Yasar, Wege zu einer Islamischen Religionspädagogik in Deutschland. In: Ucar, Bülent, Blasberg-Kuhnke, Martina, and Scheliha, Arnulf von (eds.), *Religionen in der Schule und die Bedeutung des Islamischen Religionsunterrichts*. Göttingen 2010, 191–199; Aslan, Ednan, Situation und Strömungen der islamischen Religionspädagogik im deutschsprachigen Raum. In: *Theo-Web. Zeitschrift für Religionspädagogik* (2012) 11, 10–18; Ucar, Bülent, Islamische Religionspädagogik im deutschen Kontext. Die Neukonstituierung eines alten Faches unter veränderten Rahmenbedingungen. In: Ucar, Blasberg-Kuhnke and Scheliha (eds.), *Religionen in der Schule und die Bedeutung des Islamischen Religionsunterrichts*, 33–49.

Every religion has its own specific approach to religious education, which is decisively shaped by its own sources and the context of its origin. Therefore, it is not surprising that Islam, in certain areas, has approaches and emphases in religious education that are different from those of Christianity. However, different religious pedagogical and religious didactic concepts can be found not only among the different religions, but also within the same religion.

From this point of view, the religious pedagogical or religious didactic concepts of different religions can be closer due to similar basic orientations than concepts that have arisen within a particular religion. The similarities between different religious pedagogical and religious didactic concepts of different religions are more visible, especially in worldview-religiously plural societies, such as present-day Europe, since, in pluralistic societies which have a secular, democratic and constitutional framework, all religions are equal from a legal perspective, with equal rights and obligations to the state. This common framework and the localization of Islamic religious pedagogy at secular universities constitute an important foundation for broadening horizons. Thus, it becomes possible to consider the 'dividing lines' that are too often drawn between religions and to verify whether it is rather the attitudes of the people (irrespective of their religious origin) that create the dividing lines and turn differences into unbridgeable separations. Such attitudes arise from approaches to religious content or dogma.

In a contribution that attempts to make the Innsbruck model of religious didactics fruitful for Islamic religious didactics, Sejdini states:

> There are two decisive reasons why the Innsbruck model is being consulted as a source of inspiration in this article: First, it is because, through the establishment of Islamic religious pedagogy at the University of Innsbruck, a very intensive collaboration with Catholic religious pedagogy emerged, which brought with it a closer examination of the Innsbruck model. Even more important, however, is the content orientation of the Innsbruck model, its subject- and context-relatedness. Its understanding of the truth and its communicative-theological approach are universal aspects that can also be transferred to non-Christian contexts.[71]

---

71   Sejdini, Grundlagen eines theologiesensiblen und beteiligtenbezogenen Modells, 28.

This shows that the closeness of certain attitudes, such as subject- and context-relatedness, but also the communicative-theological approach, which form the basis of interreligious religious pedagogy, are important foundations of the so-called Innsbruck model and therefore can also be applied in the interreligious context.

Consequences for an Interreligious Religious Pedagogy and Religious Didactics

In recent years, the collaboration between Islamic and Catholic Religious Pedagogy at the University of Innsbruck has grown enormously: Joint courses and joint research projects have been developed, opening up new spaces beyond their rootedness in their own religious realms. This is in keeping with our intention to consider the interreligious foundations of religious pedagogy and religious didactics on the basis of what has been worked out so far. So, in what follows, we will describe what we can take with us *together* and what we can carry *together*.

We are adopting the multiperspectivity of TCI and ComTheo, which is oriented oriented on the subject, group, content and context. This multiperspectivity presupposes a theology, religious pedagogy and religious didactics of subject, community, context and factual orientation and requires the awareness that these dimensions must not be considered in isolation, but instead must be considered in conjunction with each other. This interconnectedness of the dimensions continues in a living process of interaction among the levels, which, from immediate participation through experience and interpretation to scientific reflection, determine the increase in knowledge of (interreligious) religious pedagogy and religious didactics. Such a process cannot be conclusively planned in the longer term, as it requires constant provisional goal orientation, location determination and reorientation. As we have seen both in the example of TCI and in the foundations of ComTheo, approaches and attitudes (in the sense of the ComTheo Options) are central to the formation of religious-theological education processes. The design of multi-dimensional processes under the conditions of plurality requires an attitude of openness to possibility. Thus, we discuss, in what follows, the main features and criteria of a possibility-sensitive religious pedagogy and religious didactics before turning to the guidelines for an interreligious religious pedagogy and religious didactics.

In this context, the Innsbruck model of religious pedagogy will be re-introduced in a revised form on the basis of the empirical insight into living interreligious processes explored in volumes 2 and 3[72] of the Studies in Interreligious Religious Education series.

---

72 Kraml, Martina, Sejdini, Zekirija, Bauer, Nicole, and Kolb, Jonas, *Konflikte und Konfliktpotentiale in interreligiösen Bildungsprozessen. Empirisch begleitete Grenzgänge zwischen Schule und Universität* (Studien zur Interreligiösen Religionspädagogik, Vol. 3). Stuttgart 2020.

CHAPTER 4

Possibility-Sensitive Religious Pedagogy and Religious Didactics

So far, we have discussed the context and the anthropological, theological, educational and religious doctrinal foundations of an interreligious religious pedagogy and religious didactics from our perspectives, and in Chapter 3, we referred to our religious-pedagogical and religious-didactic origins. These concepts and experiences serve as the basis for further development. In this chapter, we deal with questions regarding our goal in developing an interreligious religious pedagogy. In the process, we pay specific attention to the possibility-suitable or contingent,[1] the understanding and religious-pedagogical significance of which seems to us to be central to the development of an interreligious religious pedagogy. Key points include the understanding of truth and the definition of interreligiosity, denominationality and identity.

What Do We Mean by 'Possibility-Sensitive'?

We have already used such concepts as possibility-suitable and contingent or contingency-sensitive, without having sufficiently clarified what we mean by them. Hence, as a first step, we wish to investigate the meaning of these concepts and, in particular, to focus our attention on the term 'contingency.'

1   Essential findings with regard to contingency and possibilities, continuity and possibility-sensitivity are taken from the post-doctoral thesis of Martina Kraml, which will be published soon: Kraml, Martina, *Dissertation gestalten im Raum der Möglichkeiten. Eine theologiedidaktische Studie zu Dissertationsprozessen mit besonderer Aufmerksamkeit auf die Entwicklung empirischer Forschung*, unveröffentlichte Habilitationsschrift. Innsbruck 2013.

What if It Were Completely Different?

There are different understandings of contingency.[2] Very often, particularly in the classical logical sense, contingency is understood as the counterpart to the concept of necessity. Two aspects of the contingent, or the possible, which is derived from it, can be characterized as follows. Aspect 1: The contingent is that which is not necessary. What is not necessary may or may not be or may be different than it is. Thereby, the possible is characterized thus: It can be different than it is. The possible, in turn, is linked to the real in some philosophical and theological schools of thought. Aspect 2: Only that which could be real is possible. In our understanding, we also differentiate and understand the possible as independent of what is real, as we will show later.[3]

Another distinction, made by Kurt Wuchterl, seems particularly fruitful for developing a contingency- and possibility-sensitive religious pedagogy and religious didactics. Wuchterl juxtaposes the *logical* or *ontological* concept of contingency (in the sense of aspect 1) with the existential contingency concept. The latter is not an objectified, 'context-less' term from the language of the logical observer, but rather a participatory or needs-related term, meaning that the contingent in the sense of the possible affects us, and influences the possibilities for our actions, our life and our education. Existential contingencies are, in Wuchterl's understanding, subjectively colored and experienced 'order breaks' that resist problem-free classification in one's own or the collective system of plausibility through reason.[4] Based on this, Wuchterl designates contingency – from a religious philosophical perspective – as 'the other of reason.'[5] At the same time, it must be added that reason and the other side of reason (that is to say, the chosen and established principles of order) can only be grasped and altered through reason. This determination of reason could be contrasted with

---

2 A very specific introduction to the history of the contingency concept can be found in: Vogt, Peter, *Kontingenz und Zufall. Eine Ideen- und Begriffsgeschichte*. Berlin 2011.

3 See Kraml, *Dissertation gestalten im Raum der Möglichkeiten*, 399–403; see also: Vogt, *Kontingenz und Zufall*, 43–66.

4 See Wuchterl, Kurt, *Kontingenz oder das Andere der Vernunft. Zum Verhältnis von Philosophie, Naturwissenschaft und Religion*. Stuttgart 2011, 11; 23–24.

5 Ibid., 11.

the view discussed in 'Reason as the Ability to Put Into Relationship' in Chapter 2. In that section, we understood reason as the ability to put in relationship. For every reasoned value assessment, one might ask, on the basis of Wuchterl's work, how the forms of correlation undertaken by humans arise. Ultimately, these forms of correlation depend on the experiences of human beings and contexts, such that over time they are 'engrained' and become habits. With an 'engrained' reason potential, however, the ability to react to new, challenges that have not yet been 'correlated' is too weak. The achievement of new relationship determination and relationship initiation is only possible when this order, in the sense of the previously correlated or previous relationship determinations, is disrupted, there is intervention, and transgressions and transcendences are possible.

This aspect of the disruptions and transcendences becomes indispensable, particularly in relation to our interreligious religious pedagogy and religious didactics: In the sense of contingency competence and plurality competence, which will be discussed later, the existing systems of order must be constantly re-thought, surpassed and extended toward other possibilities. With regard to aspect 2, the coupling of the possible with the real, there are alternative approaches. For example, the writer Robert Musil speaks, in relation to an individual human being, of the 'sense of possibility' and states that the ability to 'think about everything that could be just as good and not to take that which is, as more important than what is not.'[6]

An existential and possibility-open concept of contingency determines our interreligious religious pedagogical and religious didactic approach. In our opinion, this has considerable consequences for understanding the truth, the concept of interreligiosity and the concept of identity, which we shall discuss later.

Contingency Management, Contingency Acknowledgment, Contingency Movement

In the context of an interreligious religious pedagogy and religious didactics, a further distinction relating to dealing with contingency must

---

6   Musil, Robert, *Der Mann ohne Eigenschaften I. Erstes und zweites Buch*. Reinbek bei Hamburg 1987, 16.

be addressed. With the spread of the term contingency in the second half of the twentieth century, the concept of contingency management was coined specifically to describe the function of religion.[7] According to Kurt Wuchterl, as well as an attitude of management, an attitude of fundamental recognition of the contingent and contingency is inevitable for a life that is appropriate for humankind and its contexts. However, according to Wuchterl, it should not remain at the level of mere recognition. Rather, people are challenged to confront and encounter the contingent and contingency. Thus, Wuchterl, with a religious philosophical intention, positions the religious in the contingency *encounter* and not contingency *management*.[8]

Unlike an understanding of religion that is focused on contingency management and perceives it as a central function of religion in society, contingency acknowledgment and the contingency encounter open up new religious philosophical and theological perspectives. This religious philosophical view of contingency leads directly to theology: God, in this sense, is no longer the guarantor that contingencies will be abolished, but instead it is he who enables human recognition of contingencies and encounter initiation. We designate the recognition of contingencies and encounter initiation as contingency sensitivity and possibility sensitivity.

Focal Points of a Contingency-Sensitive Approach

The understanding of contingency, in the sense of contingency acknowledgment and contingency encounter, touches on central questions of an interreligious religious pedagogy and religious didactics. The position that one takes with regard to these questions reveals the option one has chosen: contingency denial or contingency confrontation.

7   See, for example, Hermann Lübbe's discussion of the term 'contingency management': Lübbe, Hermann, *Religion nach der Aufklärung*. Graz 1990.
8   Wuchterl, *Kontingenz oder das Andere der Vernunft*, 40–42. See also: Kraml, *Dissertation gestalten im Raum der Möglichkeiten*, 499–501.

Specific Features 'Truth' and 'Truth Claims'

In the interreligious context in particular, the concept of truth, and the claims associated with it, are continually present and are employed in argumentation or (tacitly) presupposed. This gives rise to many questions, such as the following: Is every religion 'true'? Are the 'truths' of different religions inclusive or exclusive? How can different 'truths' and truth claims coexist?

Whether interreligious collaboration, in our case interreligious religious pedagogy and religious didactics, can lead to a good life for all depends on which understanding of truth we base it on and how we deal with truth claims. Therefore, an examination of this topic in the context of a possibility-sensitive interreligious religious pedagogy and religious didactics is essential. The truth claim plays a special role in this examination: Is one's own understanding of the truth absolutized or are other approaches to the truth acknowledged?

Truth as an Ambiguous Word

First of all, it has to be taken into account that 'truth' is an ambivalent and ambiguously used word: We can discuss the truth from different scientific perspectives, such as, for example, the natural scientific, the philosophical and the theological perspectives, although in the scientific context it is not really truth that is in question, but rather correctness in the sense of the traceability and verifiability of the argumentation. Within philosophical and theological schools of thought, too, there are different theories and approaches to truth. Even individual thinkers and scientists are characterized by different and sometimes contrary approaches. Thus, objectivist approaches assume that truth is rendered recognizable and found to be static when one looks at the objective world, whereas other approaches, such as, for example, the constructivist approach, reject this, and conceive of the truth as a construct that depends on perspectives, locations, and contexts. Furthermore, like what we said in relation to contingencies in 'What if It Were Completely Different' above, one could distinguish between the truth in the philosophical logical sense (truth as a property of propositions) and truth that applies to the shaping of our lives or lifestyles as a kind of existential truth.

Our central concern in the development of an interreligious religious pedagogy is not the substantiation of truths, but rather the confrontation with the way in which truth is claimed and represented in relation to the other. Thus, questions concerning ethics and theology become relevant.

From a theological point of view, we are less concerned with the giving up on or abandoning of the claim to truth. For example, Klaus von Stosch points out that the contingency of religious convictions cannot be automatically deduced from their arbitrariness.[9] Therefore, the focus is not so much on a relativization of one's own claims to truth as on a relativization of one's own claims to absoluteness. In this context, the emphasis on contingency should make visible the limitations, fragmentedness and provisional nature of human thought and action against the background of the question of truth.

Truth Preoccupied with Power

From what has been said, it is clear that it is important to distinguish between truth and truth claims, and that claims to truth are always guided by perspectives and interests. This implies that human ways of thinking, speaking and acting in relation to truth are preoccupied with power. This 'preoccupation with power' is also present in distinctions, classifications and categorizations, which, in our opinion, are unproblematic when they are introduced and used unilaterally and with an essentialist and objectivist claim. Precisely in this seemingly plausible approach and in supposedly ordinary language systems, there is a power potential that decisively shapes living together. This power potential is activated at different times and to varying degrees, both politically and economically – for example, in right-wing political groups – by defaming other persons, groups or communities in order to characterize them as deficient and thereby enforce and legitimize the interests of those doing the defaming.

---

9 See von Stosch, Klaus, *Was sind religiöse Überzeugungen? In: Joas, Hans (ed.), Was sind religiöse Überzeugungen?* Göttingen 2003, 103–146, 139.

The Quest for Truth

A characteristic of an interreligious-sensitive existential theological concept of truth is the conviction that truth and certainty ultimately remain withheld. Milad Karimi describes this as 'truth as longing.'[10] This means that however much we speak or think about existential truth, there is always an element of the truth that cannot be detected and remains unavailable. However, this conviction of the unavailability of the truth is not simply a theoretical matter or a matter of consciousness; it is also a matter of performative action. In this way, a central moment is addressed, namely the correspondence between form and content, which is always considered with an attitude of credibility. 'True' claims can be made in a manner and with an attitude that renders them unbelievable. All forms of indoctrination fall into this area. Anyone who preaches or explains God or the truth in a way that renders the process of searching for the truth invisible and imperceptible has not grasped the truth. Such an approach is indicative of a lack of humility in relation to the truth. This humility promotes constant seeking and renders the inevitably provisional nature of the truth claim bearable.

Everything that is said here about the truth is especially valid for God as the epitome of truth. This raises the question of how we can approach this ultimate truth on the basis of the signs it reveals. The attitude we have in relation to the approach we take is of particular importance. Do we conceive of ourselves as having a claim to the truth – and thus to divine knowledge – or as constantly searching for God and therefore the truth?

---

10 Karimi, Ahmad Milad, Wahrheit ist Sehnsucht. 'So wetteifert um die guten Dinge.' In: Langthaler, Rudolf, and Tück, Jan Heiner (eds.), *'Es strebe von euch jeder um die Wette.' Lessings Ringparabel – ein Paradigma für die Verständigung der Religionen heute?* Freiburg i. Br. 2016, 278–292.

Above all, those moments of life when we are called upon by the outside and cannot control our own lives belong to this search. The following poem by Rainer Maria Rilke describes these moments:

> As long as you catch what's thrown to you, is all
> Skill and casual profit –;
> only when you suddenly become catcher of the ball,
> that the one eternal co-player
> Has thrown to you, to your center, with an exactly
> skillful momentum, in one of those arches
> from God's great bridge construction:
> only then is being able to catch a fortune, –
> not yours, of a world.[11]

Specific Feature: 'Interreligiosity'

In relation to the question of truth, the question arises of how to understand interreligiosity in the context of an interreligious religious pedagogy and religious didactics. In the first part of this section, we present different views of interreligiosity. In the second part, we open up the conceptual field. Finally, in the third part, we sketch a new understanding of denominationality.

Different Understandings of Interreligiosity

Growing plurality in Europe, and the immigration of Muslims during labor migrations in particular, gave rise to an interest in and a need for exchange between religions. In relation to the treatment of religious plurality, concepts of religious education in the plural religious context emerged very early in Great Britain. Thus, in postcolonial British society, interdenominational 'religious education' necessarily developed. This was based on a consensus between the state and the various Christian

---

11 Cited in Engel, Manfred (ed.), *Rilke–Handbuch. Leben – Werk – Wirkung.* Stuttgart 2004, 391f.

denominations. Non-Christian religions were integrated into this interdenominational 'religious education' in the 1970s.

The English religious pedagogue Michael Grimmitt outlined the fundamental distinctions between three forms of religious learning: religious learning as 'learning in religion,' 'learning about religion' and 'learning from religion.'[12] 'Learning in religion' relates to the inner perspective, while 'learning about religion' reflects the perspective of the observer. 'Learning from religion' refers to the findings of religions, which can make people more productive in their lives.

For similar reasons, in the 1960s, interest in interreligiosity also became a necessity in German-speaking countries. In this context, of the various approaches adopted, those emphasizing the encounter as an important characteristic of interreligious learning stand out.[13] Other religious pedagogues apply their interreligious religious pedagogical concepts in the framework of general education[14] and competences.[15]

Conceptual analysis of the word 'interreligious,' or the term 'interreligious learning,' must also take into account objections regarding the use of the term 'interreligious.' In particular, religious institutions[16] responsible for religious instruction and religious celebrations have concerns about the term. These concerns usually relate to too much togetherness and the mixing of traditions. For this reason, the term 'multireligious'

---

12   See Grimmitt, Michael, When is 'Commitment' a Problem in Religious Education? In: *British Journal of Educational Studies* (1981) 29, 42–53.
13   See Rickers, Folkert, Interreligiöses Lernen. In: Mette, Robert, and Rickers, Folkert (eds.), *Lexikon der Religionspädagogik*. Neukirchen-Vluyn 2001, 874–881; Kropač, Ulrich, Religiöse Pluralität als religionspädagogische Herausforderung. Perspektiven interreligiösen Lernens. In: Böttigheimer, Christoph, and Filser, Hubert (eds.), *Kircheneinheit und Weltverantwortung. Festschrift für Peter Neuner*. Regensburg 2006, 471–486; Leimgruber, *Interreligiöses Lernen*.
14   See Schweitzer, *Interreligiöse Bildung*.
15   See Schambeck, *Interreligiöse Kompetenz*.
16   See Kirchenamt der Evangelischen Kirche in Deutschland (ed.), *Klarheit und gute Nachbarschaft. Christen und Muslime in Deutschland*. Hannover 2006; Sekretariat der Deutschen Bischofskonferenz (ed.), *Leitlinien für das Gebet bei Treffen von Christen, Juden und Muslimen. Eine Handreichung der deutschen Bischöfe*. Bonn 2008.

is pushed. According to this understanding, differences are not seen as a potential way of accessing commonality, but instead as unchangeable, 'eternally divisive' characteristics. In the context of interreligious religious pedagogy, this understanding is problematic for anthropological and theological reasons. From our perspective, an understanding that contributes to an opening up and a culture of commonality, while being sensitivity to the differences, must be sought. The following considerations are intended to open up possible approaches that correspond to our understanding of interreligiosity.

From Interreligious to Transreligious?

While the term 'interreligious' is widespread in religious pedagogy and theology, the development of the cultural and educational sciences has given rise to a new challenge. In those disciplines, the prefix 'inter-' is criticized with regard to the concept of interculturality and instead the concept of transculturality is recommended. This deliberately delineates the classical concept of culture,[17] and the closed-mindedness and homogeneity with which it is associated. The notion of interculturalism, in this sense, would designate the interaction between two or more relatively closed cultural systems. Such an essentialist concept of culture and interculturality should be contrasted with 'transcultural,' possibility-open and contingency-sensitive concepts in order to leave space for a critique of cultural categorizations.

One could criticize the use of the term 'interreligiosity' for similar reasons. In this area, too, the term 'transreligious' has been brought into the conversation, albeit for a different reason.[18] The term 'transreligious' – or,

17   See Welsch, Wolfgang, 'Was ist eigentlich Transkulturalität.' In: Darowska, Lucyna, Lüttenberg, Thomas, and Machold, Claudia (eds.), *Hochschule als transkultureller Raum? Kultur, Bildung und Differenz in der Universität*. Bielefeld 2010, 39–66.
18   See Baier, Karl, Transreligiöse Theorie und existentiale Interpretation. Internet resource: <https://homepage.univie.ac.at/karl.baier/texte/pdf/Transreligioese Theorie.pdf> [accessed on February 17, 2017]; see also: Faber, Roland, Der transreligiöse Diskurs. In: *Polylog. Zeitschrift für interkulturelles Philosophieren* (2003) 9, 65–94.

perhaps better still, 'transversal'[19] – allows for and enables the identification with and discussion of the common interests that permeate religions. It also makes it possible to consider the divisions and drawbacks and to critically reflect on their effects on and consequences for one's own religion, and to consider unfamiliar forms of thought, and their distinctions and systems of differentiation, thereby discovering new possibilities.

Thus, in the context of interreligious religious pedagogy, we wish to consider the specific connotations of the terms 'transreligious' and 'transversal.' The terms imply a distancing from the idea that religions are homogeneous entities that are largely self-contained and interact with each other as such. They reflect the fact that the borders are more permeable, which should be taken into account in religious exchange. However, the term 'transreligious' could also be associated with transcending, leaving behind the living religions, which, in our view, makes it a problematic term and prevents us from using it instead of the term 'interreligious.' At the same time – in relation to the terms 'transversal' and 'transreligious' – it is worth mentioning the Indian-American literary scholar Homi K. Bhabha, who, with regard to the encounter of different cultures, speaks of a 'third space,' a term that has become established in postcolonial theories. In *The Location of Culture*[20] he analyzes the relationship between the colonizing and the colonized and discusses differences within cultural identities. For him, there is flexible interaction between cultures, because they are 'porous.' Furthermore, cultures always encounter each other in their translations, never in the original. In this context, he applies the term the 'third space,' which allows for the emergence of new positions. The 'third space' is about people of different backgrounds and attitudes negotiating new meanings. Free space is created in this process. However, the people from the weaker

19   Pope Francis, Ansprache von Papst Franziskus an den Europarat. Straßburg, Frankreich Dienstag, 25. November 2014. Internet resource: <https://w2.vatican.va/content/francesco/de/speeches/2014/november/documents/papa-francesco_20141125_strasburgo-consiglio-europa.html> [accessed on February 10, 2017]. See also: Nitsche, Bernhard, and Panikkar, Raimon, Multiple Identität als gelebte inter-intra-religiöse Transversalität. In: Bernhardt, Reinhold, and Schmidt-Leukel, Perry (eds.), *Multiple Identität. Aus verschiedenen religiösen Quellen schöpfen*. Zurich 2008, 59–78.
20   Bhabha, Homi K., *Die Verortung der Kultur*. Tübingen 2000.

culture have a protective mechanism: They seem to adapt and thus develop the possibility of resistance (a process Bhabha calls mimicry). In such a third space, the subject changes. It becomes a 'subject in motion,' a 'nomad,' 'a knotted and crossing point of languages, orders, discourses, and systems that pervade it, with all the associated perceptions, emotions, and processes of consciousness. Bhabha's metaphor of the "knotted subject" thus relocates multiculturalism, transferring it from a territorial notion to a person.'[21]

Third spaces are not specific places in territorial terms. They are processes of exchange between the unfamiliar and that which is one's own. In the third space, I change my perspective: Only by taking in another perspective, can I think about my own, can I 'cross over' in such a way that there is always a remnant that opens itself up to become a productive third space.[22]

Denominationality as the Gift of Diversity

In the analytical part of the book (Chapter 1), we highlighted the problematic aspects of the extension of the concept of denomination beyond Christian churches, especially to Islamic religious instruction. In the context of an Islamic-Christian religious pedagogy and religious didactics, the goal cannot be to eliminate the burdened concept of denomination. After all, we do not want to dissolve denominational religious instruction (in the sense of denomination-based instruction) into a general study of religion or the like, but instead to continue to think constructively, which we will endeavor to do in the following.

The notion of denominationality, which centers on the gift of diversity, reveals differences and differentiations between religions and denominations in a narrower sense. According to this understanding, the more diverse the religion is, the richer it is. However, this differentiation always

---

21   Engel, Christine, and Lewicki, Roman, Vorwort Konzepte der Interkulturalität. In: Engel, Christine, and Lewicki, Roman (eds.), *Interkulturalität. Slawistische Fallstudien.* Innsbruck 2005, 9–19, 10.

22   See Scharer, Matthias, 'Third Spaces' – Räume für interreligiöse Begegnung an 'Generativen' Themen. In: Datterl, Monika, Guggenberger, Wilhelm, and Paganini, Claudia (eds.), *Gewalt im Namen Gottes – ein bleibendes Problem?* Innsbruck 2016, 71–90.

contains a potential for conflict in the debate about the 'true' faith, which can never be voided or decided in favor of one religion. The contingent denominational potential, which, in the short term, is pushing for a 'solution' to contingency, is salutary precisely inasmuch as the recognition of abiding contingency represents an inalienable claim of religion. In this sense, institutionalized religious societies' desire for a 'normalizing' containment of denominationality in order to promote a desirable unity is problematic. This uniformity would hollow out inwardly focused diversity and thus minimize the potential for outwardly focused diversity. Those who have learned to see inwardly focused diversity as abundance will only conceive of diversity in relation to other religions and convictions.

Both in the Catholic and the Islamic spheres, a latent fear of religious ideological relativism is associated with inner and outer plurality. If many truths coexist, the uniqueness of the one truth, be it Christian or Catholic, Protestant or Islamic, could become relative. Such a fear is based on an understanding of faith that could be described as 'dogmatic': According to such an understanding, the historical struggle for the truth of faith, which can never be completed, is not appreciated. Rather, the (always contingent) results of the argument are fixed in such a way that they are deprived of the enduring openness to contingency that is part of the nature of faith. This undermines any personal or communal leeway associated with contingent faith as a life-orientation. The personal experiences that give rise to differentiation and thus pain are eliminated in this form of religious education.[23]

For people who distance themselves from church and religion, the vast differences between religious communities, inside and outside, may sometimes be incomprehensible and difficult to handle in societal and school

---

23 Pope Francis expresses the opinion that time should be given priority over space: 'To give space priority means to pretend to have solved everything in the present and to want to take possession of all spaces of power and self-affirmation. Thus, the processes will be frozen. One claims to have stopped them' (Evangelii Gaudium 223). In contrast, the precedence of time means 'setting processes in motion rather than owning spaces' (Evangelii Gaudium 223). The lasting contingency in the process of searching in life and faith is not prematurely cut off. The multitude of people and the diversity of denominations and religions are experienced as a 'spiritual' gift.

contexts. This first gives rise to the question of why different church rooms, mosques, religious rites and actions are required. Furthermore, denominational religious instruction, which is often only maintained in schools through enormous organizational effort, is difficult for many people to grasp. However, denominationality and the differences between religions, as illuminated by the secular principle of freedom *to* religion, ultimately keeps alive the problem with which a secular and, above all, neo-liberal, controlled society has to contend. This can be seen, for example, in the harmonization of diversity in favor of effective solutions, which always comes at the expense of people and a differentiated society with many different ways of life and scopes for design.

Due to societal changes, learning in and through religion, which today always means learning in the presence of the other[24] and, of course, in the presence of pupils who have no connections to church and religion, could become the model. That which unites 'people of good will' in their specific humanistic and religious traditions – even in the knowledge of their historical and enduring differences – could inspire religious teachers' and pupils' common process of searching for an existentially significant truth. It goes without saying that this must be done in an age-appropriate manner.

Specific Feature: 'Identity'

Joint processes of searching for an existentially meaningful truth, as we have suggested in the previous section, often trigger the fear that stable ego identities will be dissolved into arbitrariness, allowing an 'identity diffusion' to occur. According to Erik Erikson, whose belief it is that this is already happening, this is an enormous psychological strain for adolescents especially, because they no longer know who they are and to whom they belong. Time and again, in religious pedagogical contexts, warnings have been issued regarding the emergence of a patchwork religion, with teenagers, in particular, cobbling together their religion like a 'rag rug,'

24 Scharer, Matthias, Learning (in/through) Religion in the Presence of the Other. Accident and/or Test Case in Public Education? In: Juen, et al. (eds.), *Anders gemeinsam – gemeinsam anders?*, 223–238.

thereby dissolving their stable ego identity. Only after significant theologians, such as Raimon Panikkar,[25] spoke of a 'multiple identity' in terms of their own religiosity did a process of rethinking begin.

As early as the 1990s, the theologian Henning Luther confirmed that the effort to achieve a stable ego identity, as understood by Erikson, was already problematic for theological reasons. Such a religious pedagogical intention would obfuscate the fragmentarity that characterizes the life of every human being.[26] As a result of postmodern psychoanalytical and sociophilosophical, as well as sociological, considerations, not only was the role of attributions and affiliations in the formation of identity discovered, but the mechanisms and the inherent potential for violence of a homogeneous understanding of identity were also made clear. In everyday life, the concept of identity is repeatedly used in politics, but also in religion, as a means of demarcating or excluding others or those who are unfamiliar.

In recent decades, plural ways of life and new social developments, such as mobility and migration movements, have contributed to a problematization of the notion of identity and a reflection on the relationship between plurality and identity. People who value plurality will have a different understanding of identity than people for whom plurality poses a threat. Naturally, plurality in society and within and outside religions initially gave rise to uncertainty and confusion. Adequate forms of interaction had to be found.

The concept of perspectivity is geared toward an appropriate approach to plurality. The adoption of perspectivity was connected to a reorientation in the previous paradigm landscape: The line of vision moved away from the static and immutable toward movement and change, utilizing metaphors of the border, the transitory, etc. Stronger relationships and relations were favored over fixed locations, and an overarching or objectivist viewpoint was replaced by perspectivity as a suitable means for adequately moving in plurality, theoretically and practically. In this regard, Kurt Röttgers writes:

---

25 See Nitsche and Panikkar, Multiple Identität als gelebte inter-intra-religiöse Transversalität.
26 See Luther, *Religion und Alltag*, 62–87.

> Mediation, in other words, an allocating center, is imperative solely due to the inexplicable perspective for no one sees everything at once, or finds him or herself simultaneously in this world and the hereafter. Because, as I have said, unfamiliarity is not a phenomenal finding, but rather a classification category.[27]

In order to face the societal conditions of plurality and its challenges, a wealth of philosophical, theological, pedagogical and other concepts have been developed. Of interest in this context is the concept of 'transitory identity,'[28] in which the 'process character of modern personal self-relations'[29] is the center of attention. According to Straub and Renn, self-relations are not stable, but rather subject to contingency and therefore to movement. Thus, the relationship to the self, in the sense of identity in transition, must be established and proven.[30] Other notions of identity that emerged included 'religious multilingualism'[31] and 'multiple religious identities,'[32] which, when lived authentically, lead to transitions and transversals, to encounters in border spaces.[33] Manuela Kalsky developed the idea of 'religious flexibility.'[34] She states:

> The boundaries of what we call identity are becoming ever more permeable and fluid both in the personal and societal sphere. The accompanying changes do not occur without internal and external conflicts. While some find the loss of fixed identities threatening and resort to former traditions in their search for support, for others the

27 Röttgers, Kurt, *Identität als Ereignis. Zur Neufindung eines Begriffs*. Bielefeld 2016, 333f.
28 Renn, Joachim, and Straub, Jürgen, Der Prozesscharakter moderner personaler Selbstverhältnisse. In: Straub, Jürgen, and Renn, Joachim (eds.), *Transitorische Identität. Der Prozesscharakter des modernen Selbst*. Frankfurt a. Main 2002, 10–31, 10.
29 Ibid.
30 Ibid., 23–29.
31 Bernhardt, Reinhold, 'Synkretismus' als Deutekategorie für multireligiöse Identitätsbildungen. In: Bernhardt, Reinhold, and Schmidt-Leukel, Perry (eds.), *Multiple religiöse Identität. Aus verschiedenen religiösen Traditionen schöpfen*. Zurich 2008, 267–290, 278.
32 Ibid., 290.
33 Nitsche and Panikkar, Multiple Identität als gelebte inter-intra-religiöse Transversalität, 77.
34 Kalsky, Manuela, Religiöse Flexibilität. Eine Antwort auf kulturelle und religiöse Vielfalt. In: Bernhardt and Schmidt-Leukel (eds.), *Multiple religiöse Identität*, 219–242.

dissolution of established identities, and the cultural and religious roles that they impose, is a relief from oppressive structures.[35]

Karl Baier distinguishes four elements for understanding identity: 1) cognitive self-perception: what someone thinks about him- or herself, 2) emotional self-perception: that which one feels, 3) the perception of others: the perception of what others think of one, 4) self-perception: perception of one's own actions.[36]

An important aspect in the context of the concept of identity is fear, or panic, when one understands this as fear in a heightened form. There is a range of phenomena that counteract those anthropological aspects we have already mentioned, such as human dignity, freedom, reason and responsibility, or interfere with or complicate the targeted relationship determinations. One of them is fear. Martha Nussbaum characterizes the time in which we live as a time of fear and suspicion.[37] Neither fear nor suspicion is unique to this era. Throughout the centuries, subjective and collective fear and suspicion have arisen. Fear is a fundamental anthropological phenomenon with many facets.

Transferences and projections constitute another important subject in the context of identity and identity formation. Both fundamentally shape verbal and non-verbal communication and, along with other fundamental transferences, help us to navigate and communicate in the world.

> We fall back on past adventures and experiences in new situations, in order not to have always to start afresh and without any previous knowledge, so to speak, from zero point. If our brain did not constantly recapitulate, we would be overwhelmed by fears of the unknown and the new, on the one hand, and on the other hand, we would not be able to make any progress because this can only build on what is already available and what has already been learned. Thirdly, we could not communicate because we would have nothing that we could relate to together.[38]

---

35 Ibid., 239f.
36 See Baier, Karl, Spiritualität und Identität. In: Bernhardt and Schmidt-Leukel (eds.), *Multiple religiöse Identität*, 187–218, 201.
37 Nussbaum, Martha, *Die neue Intoleranz. Ein Ausweg der Politik aus der Angst*. Darmstadt 2014, 12–26.
38 Rubner, Angelika, and Rubner, Eike, *Unterwegs zur funktionierenden Gruppe. Die Gestaltung von Gruppenprozessen mit der Themenzentrierten Interaktion*. Gießen 2016, 69.

In the case of transferences, elements of other situations, even unpleasant situations that troubled us, are transferred to a new situation. When we are in a situation in which we feel exposed, and we are suddenly reminded of another similar situation from the past, we transfer the feelings from one to the other. This can also occur in relation to people. A particular face, posture or voice can remind us of another person that we have experienced positively or negatively. Transferences can be positive or negative. Either way, they have a significant impact on our communication. The elucidation of one's own life story helps one to deal constructively with the inevitable transferences and thereby get one's own subjective models and concepts on track. Such 'elucidation work' is a prerequisite for changing one's attitude. In the interreligious context, it is not only childhood transitions that play a role; we often have to deal with everyday transferences from adults, who generalize what they have heard or experienced without further reflection and transfer it to individual people or entire groups.

By 'projection,' we mean, in the psychological sense, those inner images, feelings and aspirations that we have absorbed since childhood, and, although we may not like to admit it, that we project onto other people. This happens, for example, when we struggle internally with moral or religious taboos, because the conflict between what we would like to do and what we should do has not been argued out and we have not clarified what we really want. The projection of such unprocessed taboos, desires and aspirations onto other people can be the cause of anxiety in relation to strangers and can severely hamper open communication.

Consequences for an Interreligious Religious Pedagogy and Religious Didactics

Diversity is a reality, in nature, as well as in society and religion. In this context, the task of interreligious religious pedagogy and religious didactics is primarily to strengthen contingency sensitivity and diminish contingency management. This can make it easier to deal with a contingent world and render the potential of educational processes more fruitful.

An adequate handling of contingency is only possible in the context of an understanding of truth claims that does not exclude other truth claims and does not absolutize one's own claim. The notion of interreligiosity reveals that terminologies are not neutral, but rather reflect concepts that have political implications. When we speak, we include or exclude. This means that even the concept of interreligiosity cannot be restricted to a dialogue of delimited, self-contained constructions of religion and must rather transcend previous constructions and open up new spaces.. In conclusion, as Henning Luther writes in relation to identity: 'Religious education should not have a fixed identity ideal attached to its goal, but rather the ability to transcend set patterns of life.'[39]

---

39 Luther, *Religion und Alltag*, 59.

CHAPTER 5

Possibility-Suitable Conceptualizations of Interreligious Educational Processes

In Chapter 4 we introduced the terms 'possibility-sensitive' and 'possibility-suitable,' meaning that 'something can also be different to how it is currently.' This chapter seeks to render the foundations of a possibility-suitable religious pedagogy and religious didactics fruitful for the conceptualization of interreligious educational processes. No particular religious-pedagogical and religious-didactic concept is pursued, for we are still at the level of contours. In the following volumes in this series, a concept of interreligious religious pedagogical collaboration is developed using evidence-based processes.[1]

In what follows, we will outline the fundamentals, in the form of guidelines. Thereafter, we will discuss different approaches to religious pedagogical and religious didactic action.

Religious Pedagogical and Religious Didactic Guidelines

The goal of a religious pedagogy or a religious didactics is to develop theoretical and practical principles for professional didactic action. On the one hand, didactic action is about gaining confidence in planning, leadership and teaching, so that appropriate learning opportunities can be offered to all participants, the learners and the teachers, skills can be promoted and appropriated, and certain standards can be achieved. At the same time, we are skeptical about the urge to consistently standardize

[1] See Kraml and Sejdini (eds.), *Interreligiöse Bildungsprozesse*; Kraml, Sejdini, Bauer and Kolb, *Konflikte und Konfliktpotentiale in interreligiösen Bildungsprozessen*.

possible interreligious competences.[2] This is because 'the best of religion cannot be standardized' and because, especially in interreligious learning situations, descriptions of plans, goals and competences, which seem appropriate at first, often have to be spontaneously changed and adapted over and over again. For example, 're-planning in the process,' as it is referred to in TCI, is an everyday occurrence in interreligious learning processes and requires a high degree of teaching and leadership competence. That which was neither premeditated nor planned can become, at the right moment, the so-called *kairos* of the learning process. The fact that it is only in the living and current communication of a study group that a claim to truth can suddenly become apparent, which can lead to a power gap and obscure the common search for existential truth, poses a great didactic challenge to the attention competence for processes and to the spontaneous re-planning competence and leadership of learning processes. A theme- and process-conscious, multiperspective didactic approach, based on the attitude we have attempted to articulate in this book, forms, in our opinion, the basis of interreligious professionalism.

Theme Orientation and Process Orientation

As a rule, didactic planning is based on a ready-made scheme. For interreligious learning processes, only a process-oriented planning scheme that serves the orientation of the teachers and leaders and takes a possibility-suitable and contingency-sensitive stance is helpful. Themes and processes play a crucial role in such schemes.

As discussed in the section on Ruth C. Cohn's theme-centered interaction ('Theme-Centered Interaction and the Concept of Communicative Theology' in Chapter 3), existentially important themes are the core of living learning processes. This is especially true for interreligious learning. The themes are not just formulated content, learning objects, goals, or competences, as they are in official curricula, but nor are they completely

2   Englert, Rudolf, Bildungsstandards für Religion. Was eigentlich wissen sollte, wer solche formulieren wollte. In: Sajak (ed.), *Bildungsstandards für den Religionsunterricht – und nun*, 9–28.

independent of these. We regard official curricula or syllabi as a pool of possible content-related aspects of the teaching or learning process, from which a selection is to be made. The more qualitative they are, the more deeply they reveal both the scientific anchoring and the situational and context-related significance of the learning objects and the goals and competences. By contrast, standardized competence formulations have an orientation function and are intended to highlight the 'initiation moment' of learning processes, whereby possibility-suitability and contingency sensitivity can also guide the concrete learning process in another direction or make other emphases appear more necessary than they are currently thought or expected to be.

Even if a curriculum, for whatever didactic field, is formulated in a deeply substantiated and participatory way, by adequately describing goals and competences, for example, these never depict the learning process itself, that is, concrete processes of learning. Those who forget this advocate for an application-oriented religious pedagogy and religious didactics, which we want to counteract with this book. So if not the curriculum itself, what can guide a learning process?

We believe that existentially important themes, which are deeply relevant and immediately perceptible to the participants, a concrete context-relatedness and an interaction/communication stimulus, form the core of living interreligious learning processes. According to Matthias Kroeger, theme formulations in the field of religious pedagogy offer 'themes that are disregarded, unsocialized, and persistently devoid of language and consciousness [note: in our view, this is a matter of concern] means of expression.'[3]

The art of finding and formulating such themes and introducing them into the learning process requires a high level of competence in the subject and in verbalization, as well as a pronounced sensitivity regarding the respective interaction and communication experience. The great advantage of the theme-orientation of learning processes is that the situational openness and appropriateness of interreligious learning, called for in this book, can actually be achieved.

3   Kroeger, *Themenzentrierte Seelsorge*, 213.

Even though it might seem to be the case because of the far-reaching competences that are required of theme leaders or teachers, there is nothing unapproachable or complicated about the learning process. On the contrary: In our everyday life, we constantly communicate in relation to themes, when our communication does not slide into small talk, during which nothing more (of significance) is said. But even small talk (particularly more formal small talk) could be focused on and led back to an existentially significant communication.

In this context, we must always assume that in learning groups, especially interreligious ones, there is a high degree of theme diversity, as well as theme rivalry. It should be remembered that even that which is 'under the carpet' and not openly addressed constitutes theme material. The more likely a subject is to be forgotten or obscured, the more meaningful it usually is as a theme for discussion. Thus, so-called disruptions[4] have great potential. When they can be 'retrieved from under the carpet' and discussed, they lead to in-depth learning activities.

The same applies to so-called shadow themes that represent the taboo side of official themes, which are mostly taken from the curricula. In particular, resistance on the part of the learners to an official theme and to its spontaneous situation-appropriate reformulation, which includes and focuses on the resistance, opens up interreligious learning opportunities, which can actually lead learners further and prevent unauthentic communication. It should be borne in mind that discussions of difficult issues should not necessarily occur at the beginning of an interreligious learning process, since trust must first be allowed to develop.

When themes become the center of living learning processes, they point the way for learning activities and serve to guide them. This means that the theme must be clarified in advance, including both its concrete formulation and the means for its introduction, before a learning process is structured, a process which includes determining the forms of work, methods and media. Simultaneously, however, as implied above, the subject matter may change in the process, necessitating a spontaneous reformulation by

---

4   See 'Theme-Centered Interaction and the Concept of Communicative Theology' in Chapter 3.

the leader or the group of learners as a whole. Only when such thematic interventions are recognized as necessary and are introduced competently, boldly and sometimes aggressively by the leaders does the learning process remain oriented and alive rather than becoming an ultimately routine activity that is therefore devoid of meaning, as frequently occurs in schools, colleges and other educational institutions.

Theme orientations and process orientations interact directly in our didactic concept, in which theme clarification, including its precision, brevity, attractiveness and existential importance, is prioritized in process planning. If the theme is clear, the process planning steps are usually very simple. Of course, theme clarification alone cannot compensate for didactic skill and experience, since these must also to be determined based on the topic and situation. The above-mentioned competences in 'revision in the process' or discussion of 'shadow themes,' which require extensive experience and practice in theme-based learning, can initiate interreligious learning processes in a specific way.

Diversity and Multiperspectivity

As was made clear in Chapter 4, contingency is the cause of plurality. Dealing with plurality brings with it the ability to handle contradictions and ambivalences. As we noted, educational institutions face major future challenges in relation to their appreciative and sensitive approach to contingency, plurality and ambivalence. This task is particularly relevant to interreligious religious pedagogy and religious didactics. Thus, under the conditions of contingency, plurality, ambiguity and ambivalence, it is no longer appropriate to orient oneself by means of ready-made and context-independent categories and models. Rather, according to Martin Fuchs, 'principles of action and [...] interpretation can only be classified "in practice" in the context of social interactions.'[5]

---

5   Fuchs, Martin, Das Ende der Modelle: Interkulturalität statt (Kultur-)Vergleich. Cited in: Holzinger, Markus, *Kontingenz der Gegenwartsgesellschaft. Dimensionen eines Leitbegriffs moderner Sozialtheorie.* Bielefeld 2007, 331f.

If one understands this in the context of interreligious religious pedagogy and religious didactics, it is clear that linear and one-dimensional models, which are based solely on content, are no longer appropriate for the current development of science and society. As indicated in the previous section, it is necessary to adopt an attitude that there is still something else possible other than what currently manifests itself. Such an attitude 'does not fall from the sky.' It is the task of education to shape it. In the words of Markus Holzinger, one could speak here of the necessity of 'practicing the sense of possibility.'[6] Interreligious education would thus be a place of communicative action, in which the fear of diversity, contradictions and ambivalence could be broken down and a constructive interaction with others could be learned. In the process of learning, reflexivity and the confrontation with other approaches, life experiences and perspectives are important. At the same time, the awareness of perspectivity and the diversity of perspectives, as well as the handling of them, prove to be decisive starting points.

The approaches of multiperspectivity and the networking of perspectives, as characterized by TCI, ComTheo and the Innsbruck model of religious didactics, are central starting points for the further development of the interreligious religious didactic conceptualization. This multi-perspective approach can be used as a process-oriented instrument for working on reflection on and the changing of perspectives, as well as on the issues of diversity in educational contexts.

Language Sensitivity and Discrimination Sensitivity

In several sections (for example, 'Immigration Society' in Chapter 1), we have already addressed the problem of the 'asymmetric perspective,' also referred to as 'asymmetric hermeneutics' or overemphasis[7] on differences and categorizations, for example, in the context of the majority/minority

6   Ibid., 332.
7   Mecheril, Paul, 'Kompetenzlosigkeitskompetenz'. Pädagogisches Handeln unter Einwanderungsbedingungen. In: Auernheimer, Georg (ed.), *Interkulturelle Kompetenz und pädagogische Professionalität*. Wiesbaden 2010, 15–34, 21.

society, and its far-reaching effects and implications and their concealment through ontologization and naturalization, religiously justified or not.

Thus, we find in the work of Rose Nadin an example in the form of a teacher's evaluation of a particular student's German assignment. The student exerted considerable effort to improve and had seen great progress in his work; the teacher's feedback is 'not so bad for a foreigner.'[8] The impact of this feedback can only be discouraging. It contains little information regarding actual performance, rather implying that the student's performance is related to his minority status, which is connoted as deficient. The feedback thus contains a pejorative attitude in relation to the constructed social attribution.

Conversely, non-discrimination, in the sense of no emphasis on difference, can have inclusive effects: The 4-year-old Niklas, who happens to come upon the scene of an interview with rapper Fard for the show *hiphop. de*, is asked by Fard how he feels in the daycare center and whether there are foreigners. Niklas responds: 'No, there are children.'[9] The inclusive impact of language becomes clear in this particular context. It is not differences that are meaningful or life-necessary, but their 'diffusion' in the shared state of being a child. Of course, this non-differentiation could also have problematic consequences if, for example, the unfavorable status of foreigners was not recognized and dealt with, since no differentiation was made.

One of the special challenges of the interreligious conceptualization of educational processes consists therefore of critical reflection on the inclusive or exclusive effects of speech and action language patterns, in particular dualistic-binary concepts.[10]

---

8   Rose, Nadine, 'Für 'nen Ausländer gar nicht mal schlecht'. Zur Interpretation von Subjektbildungsprozessen in Migrationsbiographien. In: Mecheril, Paul (ed.), *Subjektbildung. Interdisziplinäre Analysen der Migrationsgesellschaft*. Bielefeld 2014, 57–77.
9   We were made aware of this example by Erol Yildiz. See Focus online, Ein Vierjähriger liefert die perfekte Antwort auf die Flüchtlingsfrage. Vier Worte genügten. Internet resource: <http://www.focus.de/politik/deutschland/vier-worte-genuegten-dieser-vierjaehrige-beantwortet-die-fluechtlingsfrage-ziemlich-schlagfertig_id_4883387.html> [accessed on March 1, 2017].
10 Josef Mitterer deals with dualistic epistemological patterns in his works. See Mitterer, Josef, *Die Flucht aus der Beliebigkeit*. Weilerswist 2011, 107–118.

In this context, Paul Mecheril's statement regarding the need to classify 'racism-critical religious pedagogy' must be taken into consideration.[11] The starting point for such a racist-critical emancipatory religious pedagogy, which in this case must be very sensitive to Islamophobic, anti-Christian and anti-Semitic utterances and attitudes, is a critical view of one's own perspective and self-generated language and thought constructs, as well as the self-constructed 'big' and 'small' narratives or discourses, which reflect societal circumstances and could develop into stereotypes, such as 'good religion – evil religion.'

Conversely, members of the minority society (such as, for example, Muslims) should also deal with their own asymmetrical patterns or stereotypes vis-à-vis the majority society. Members of the minority society possess their own prejudices and specific attitudes, and, in many cases, are prepared to critically review their own expectations, particularly as a high percentage of Muslims come to European countries by choice.

'Incompetence Competence'[12]

The previous sections of this chapter have repeatedly raised the question of competences, which plays an important role in the current religious-didactic discussion. In order to demonstrate that competence orientation is legitimate in some ways, but should not be used uncritically, especially in an interreligious context, the comments that follow not only affirmatively consider competence logic, but also problematize it in the interreligious field and, in particular, critically reflect on its communicative effects.

At this point, the question also arises of asymmetrical 'logics'[13] or concepts and power relations (in the sense of perspective, interpretation and action dominance), which are (in most cases implicitly) focused on in discussions of competence orientation. When it comes to asymmetrical

---

11 Lingen-Ali and Mecheril, Religion als soziale Deutungspraxis, 22.
12 Mecheril, 'Kompetenzlosigkeitskompetenz,' 15.
13 The term 'logic' is used here as it is in everyday language, in the sense of cognitive constructs or concepts.

logics and power relations, the lack of reflection on competence orientation is striking. Mecheril addresses this question in the context of intercultural competences by highlighting asymmetries using the example of corresponding educational opportunities, and by pointing out that opportunities are almost always made available to members of the majority society. 'Nor do [they] seem to find any occasion to thematize the egalitarian hypothesis, which is committed to approaches to cultural difference, in order to discuss contradictory non-consideration.'[14]

Likewise, according to Mecheril, such opportunities and concepts are generally based on unconscious stereotypes and implied power relations in the context of interreligious education: Communication most often emanates from majority members, and is aimed in the direction of the minority. The majority locates deficits in the minority society (an inability to integrate, etc.) and in the dealings of majority members with minority members. These deficits should be 'handled' as professionally as possible. Education, professional training and continuing education programs are seen as tools to remedy these shortcomings. Mecheril highlights the instrumentalization of education and the role of an instrumentalized and functionalized concept of competence. In particular, religious and interreligious education is to be intensively considered in relation to the extent to which it contains asymmetrical stereotypes that make members of minority society objects of education, the extent to which the concept of competence supports this and the extent to which the concept of competence in intercultural or interreligious contexts is based on feasibility fantasies. Here, too, it is important to warn against an 'instrumental understanding of intercultural competence, which primarily focuses on the socio-technical utilization of knowledge about cultures and their identifiable characteristics.'[15] To name and work on this problem, Paul Mecheril introduces the term 'incompetency-competence.' This means the need for reflection on the capacity of the concept of competence, its conceptual and communicative effects, its opportunities and limitations, and the recognition of its boundaries, especially in view of the 'technology-deficit' of (religious) pedagogical and (religious) didactic

---

14   Mecheril, 'Kompetenzlosigkeitskompetenz,' 17.
15   Ibid.

action. With regard to interreligious religious pedagogy and religious didactics, it is important to learn from migration pedagogy and to always reflect on and discuss together where the competence concept creates, amplifies, suppresses or harmonizes imbalances and asymmetries.

Attitudes in Religious Pedagogical and Religious Didactic Action

In the first chapter, we addressed our biographical foundations, and, relatedly, we discussed the contexts of educational processes. Chapters 2 and 3 were dedicated to the anthropological and theological foundations, as well as the foundations of education and the paradigms that have guided us until now. In Chapter 4 we addressed possibility sensibility and contingency sensitivity as important characteristics, from our point of view, for interreligious religious pedagogy and religious didactics. From all this, it has become clear that interreligious encounter, communication and reflection is not methodical matter. It is necessary, rather, to practice and cultivate a particular attitude. Thus, following religious pedagogical and religious didactic guidelines, we will consider attitudes that are conducive to a fluid concept of interreligious religious pedagogy and religious didactics. In the following, we will discuss three basic features of such attitudes.

He Who Never Leaves his Shore Cannot Discover Anything New

One of the most important attitudes in the field of interreligious religious pedagogy and religious didactics is certainly openness to the other, the unknown and the supposedly unfamiliar, for undoubtedly one of the conditions for learning is the necessity of mustering the courage to look beyond one's own nose. This attitude is therefore associated with courage, because it can create a sense of insecurity, incompleteness and unpredictability in relation to religion or belief. Even though this 'vacillation with regard to the individual' is indispensable for education in a plural context, it is frequently viewed as deficient. This is particularly the case in some religious and philosophical-theological contexts, which promote themselves as a 'solid ground' of unquestionable individual competence and a unique and irrefutably secure body of knowledge, which distinguishes itself from others in every respect and therefore implicitly devalues others.

However, in an interreligious religious pedagogy and religious didactics, the willingness to leave one's own shore is a basic prerequisite for fruitful collaborative work. This attitude makes it possible to get to know and understand the other, but also to be able to see religion or belief from the perspective of new experiences, and thus to recognize the potential or the limitedness of one's own perspective, for only when 'other continents' are discovered can 'one's own shore' be adequately considered and categorized: The one who has left his or her shore and found new opportunities for living in the midst of religious and ideological diversity will be able to marvel at the plurality of conceptions of life and religious approaches as an expression of aliveness, and he or she will enjoy it as a special gift of God. At the same time, one sometimes feels that one has left an old home and entered unknown territory. This can be frightening and can lead to loneliness. There is a big difference between those who think they know everything about religions and worldviews, but who, despite that knowledge, end up in the 'safe haven' of their own beliefs, and those who engage existentially with new experiences in the direct encounter with people from other religions and with other convictions.

We contrast the attitude of knowing everything (*about* the other) in interreligious encounters and preferably keeping it easy to grasp, with the attitude that is aptly described with the metaphor 'living in the border country.' Michael Nausner, influenced by Homi K. Bhabha, the 'Father of the Third Space,' whom we have already mentioned, has written an essay on this metaphor, which he initially locates within Christianity. Nausner has dual citizenship (Austrian and Swedish) and is 'a non-American clergyman in a paradigmatic American faith community (the Methodist Church).'[16] Against the background of the multiple difficulties that he has with the

---

16 Nausner, Michael, Heimat als Grenzland. Territorien christlicher Subjektivität. In: Nehring, Andreas, and Tielesch, Simon (eds.), *Postkoloniale Theologien. Bibelhermeneutische und kulturwissenschaftliche Beiträge*. Stuttgart 2013, 187–202, 188.

word 'home,' particularly when it is connected to religion, he finds himself following the Protestant theologian P. Tillich into the border region. Tillich has lived with the fact that 'our home is in a sense always on the border.'[17]

Borders, even boundaries between denominations and religions, do not need to be interpreted as rigidly delimiting; they can be understood much more dynamically as opening up new spaces and possibilities. To move in the borderland, even to consider the borderland to be one's actual homeland, transcends the borders of the other and undermines the superiority of putting oneself above the other. This attitude, which opens up new spaces in the borderland, is by no means free of fear. The encounter with the other is always a risk, especially in the interreligious realm. Regardless of the good will involved, excessive truth and control claims could hurt or silence the other. The experience of being able to be in one's own religion and among those of us who are at home in different religions could be quite different to what most people would expect and maybe even different to what I would expect myself; it could overwhelm me and others. Living in the borderland is therefore a risk with a highly uncertain outcome.

Inspired by the anthropologist Sam Gill, who conducted research on the Aborigines in Australia, Nausner draws a different picture to that of delimitation and enclosure. Borderland, in the Aboriginal sense, is not a closed territory or spiritual space, such as most people would associate with the concept of home: It is a network with tracks and footprints around it, including those of the ancestors. Nausner, in taking up research on the Aborigines, is not concerned with a postmodern glorification of nomadic life forms, with their alternative attitude toward the demarcated territories of the sedentary. Instead he points out that a community can no longer assume 'that cultures, ideologies or territories are a homogeneous whole that must be clearly divided up.'[18]

The attitude associated with life in the 'unknown territory' of the borderland, which correlates with experiences of the Third Space, as described by Bhabha, does not shy away from risk, even when confronted with all the

---

17   Ibid., 191.
18   Ibid., 202.

fears associated with it, but instead is courageous enough to approach the unknown and new, which facilitates the encounter of religions.

Encountering One Another with Respect, with One Another Instead of Above One Another, at Eye Level

For us, the starting point of interreligious religious pedagogy and religious didactics is an attitude of openness to encounter. In the empathetic person-to-person encounter, one finds what one refers to as concerning oneself with one another: The awareness of one's own situation and compassion in joy and sorrow enable a solidary encounter beyond individual, political and social life social norms and prejudices. Through this conscious encounter, which is always considered afresh, authentic teaching and learning are enabled and tolerance, respect for the other, and recognition of the other are promoted. This kind of encounter, however, gives rise not only to harmony. Differences also become visible and conflicts can arise. Dealing with conflicts requires the formation and development of special attitudes and competences, such as respect and empathy, in teacher education, as well as in the classroom and educational action fields. Martha Nussbaum speaks of 'respect and compassionate fantasy'[19] in the sense of 'inner eyes'[20] when it comes to meeting people of other religions, and states that these inner eyes are not always sufficiently developed to cope with the cares and pleasures of the other, or to be able to perceive and accept the concerns and values of the other. We believe that education must aim to shape and develop the attitude of the inner eye.

If one wants to describe an encounter as appreciative and acknowledging, one frequently uses another eye metaphor, namely 'eye level.' In an eye-level encounter, the human-existential aspect also resonates. Such an encounter does not involve distancing, or talking about, but rather 'talking to the other.' This is associated with an attitude of openness to and interest in the other, which opens up the same spaces to others and grants them

---

19 Nussbaum, *Die neue Intoleranz*, 120–155.
20 Ibid., 120f.

opportunities that one would like to have granted to oneself. The expression 'eye level' also includes an invitation to participate. It connotes a culture of mutual recognition, participation and cooperation (along with all the possible competition that goes with life and work). The encounter, the joint learning at eye level, does not involve the obfuscation of the roles of teachers and learners. Rather, it is possible to recognize the different roles and face each other on an essentially human-existential level.

In interreligious religious educational and didactic teaching and research, questions arise about the feasibility of this eye-level encounter between teachers and students. In order to facilitate this kind of encounter, the collective development of appropriate concepts from kindergarten to university is a necessity. The further development of scientific-theoretical and methodological approaches to interreligious teaching and research must continue.

Taking Part, Participation, Opening Up Spaces

That which was addressed in the previous section can be considered a prerequisite for this section. 'Inner eyes,' as they relate to respect, interest and empathy, are attentive to possibilities for the other/the others to take part or participate. We must ask ourselves how we allow the other/the others to take part or participate, what possibilities and spaces we, as Christians or Muslims or otherwise faithful people, open up for the other and how we understand these forms of involvement. There is a reason why we distinguish between taking part and participating. This distinction relates to different kinds of involvement in forms of prayer and celebration for which people of different religions gather. An example in which the distinction between taking part and participating plays an important role is prayer, festivals or celebrations in schools with religious orientations.

Above all, one finds in schools different forms, in which time and again religions are also involved: 1) 'Intrareligious' prayers and celebrations: religious celebrations of a particular religious community (*participating in one's own*) in which members of other religious communities take part (*taking part in the religion of the other*). Here we can observe that it is usually majority Christian celebrations that take place, with others, such as Muslims, for example, taking part – implicitly and often in an unexplained role – whereas, for example, there are hardly any Muslim 'intrareligious' prayers and celebrations in schools that are attended by Christian or non-denominational pupils. 2) There are also 'collective' religious prayers, celebrations or festivals, with different, shared or separate parts for different religions. 3) Among the various prayers and celebrations that take place in schools, there are collective celebrations that are purported to be fundamentally religious, but are actually aimed at general human concerns, such as peace, justice, etc., so the pupils of the religious communities that are represented take part or participate in a similar way.

Within Christianity, as already indicated in 'Specific Attributes of 'Interreligiosity' in Chapter 4, where 'joint' religious celebrations are concerned (Type 2), there has been a broad discussion about the use of the word 'interreligious.' Such prayers or celebrations are often viewed with skepticism and reservations in Christian church contexts. There is a fear of too much 'mutuality' and thus mixing. To avoid this danger, the term 'multireligious' has been suggested in order to emphasize the demarcation between the prayer forms of the various religions more clearly.[21] It has also been highlighted that the theological prerequisites for 'interreligious' celebrations are lacking or have not been sufficiently clarified. Hence, there is a danger of giving the impression of a 'universal religion,' which must be avoided. Thus, according to this stance, it is not a question of joint prayer, but rather the prayers of different religions in the same place.

When presented with justifications for differentiating between religions, particularly in relation to their performative acts, such as prayer and religious celebrations, we reflect critically on the attitude behind the meticulous attempts at differentiation and demarcation. It is also necessary to query the understanding of God that is articulated.

Thus, the task of religious pedagogy and religious didactics, even theological pedagogy and didactics, is connected to the search for a humane

---

21 Kirchenamt der Evangelischen Kirche in Deutschland (EKD) (ed.), *Klarheit und gute Nachbarschaft. Christen und Muslime in Deutschland.* Hannover 2006, 117; Schulamt der Diözese Innsbruck (ed.), *Miteinander Feiern in der Schule. (Religiöse) Feiern im multireligiösen Schulkontext.* September 2016.

form of co-existence that involves the other in an appropriate manner, with respect and esteem. This poses the following questions: Who determines the rules of the game for this 'being together'? Which asymmetries and power relations become visible – on both sides – in the execution of these rules?

It turns out that the 'intrareligious' prayers and festivals of a religious community in which others are involved pose a particular question about the transparency of the roles and the forms of participation. Is it made clear, for example, that Muslims are present at a Christian festival in a different – participatory – way than Christians are? And vice versa? Are Muslim festivals, among others, honored in educational institutions such as schools and kindergartens, so that Muslim pupils can also experience being in an authentic, participatory and contributing role?[22] As long as everything goes routinely, the danger of reproducing old prejudices and stereotypes, old asymmetries and power relations in both directions – from the members of the majority society, that is, the Christians, toward the members of the minority society, for example, Muslims, and vice versa – continues to exist. New third-party spaces are hardly possible where routine is maintained. Mostly, it is the fruits of contingency, the 'stumbling blocks,' the disturbances that cause things to go 'out of step' and make new beginnings possible. Such events upset the previous task and role allocation, creating new arrangements and thus new forms of taking part and participation. These questions bring us into new territory. Hence we need the empathetic imagination, in the sense of fantasy and creativity, that we discussed in the previous chapter.

In summary, where guidelines and attitudes are concerned, it becomes clear that it is above all the open-heartedness, generosity and solidarity of religious and secular people that are necessary in order to make possible human and substantive approaches, which are a precondition for approaching God. At the same time, we should be aware in two ways: In the 'Globe,' which surrounds us all, with the challenges it presents; and in the concern not to lose sight of the good life for all people here and hereafter and to be in solidarity with and bear good will toward all people. These

22 See Peter, Teresa, 'Ich stehe vor Dir.' Die Bedeutung von spirituellem Anteilnehmen-Lassen und Anteil-Nehmen im Dialog. In: Kästle, Kraml and Mohagheghi (eds.), *Heilig-Tabu*, 215–220.

Possibility-Suitable Conceptualizations

attitudes are fed by sources that we all find in our traditions, especially in the mystical expressions of our traditions. Martha Nussbaum speaks of the 'inner mind, which must enliven the search for a consistent attitude, should this not remain an empty shell.'[23]

---

23   Nussbaum, *Die religiöse Intoleranz*, 197.

Epilogue

The themes covered in this book relate to a spiritual depth that is beyond the reach of knowledge and competence. Without this spiritual depth, interreligious religious pedagogy and religious didactics seem superficial. Therefore, we have decided to end the book with a conversation with a shaman who, we believe, expresses our concern very well:

> Question: Why should one take a spiritual path if one ends up with the knowledge that one knows nothing? Shaman: There is a beauty in this kind of ignorance. It is a conscious ignorance and not an oblivious one. And over time, you get to a point where you indulge in the idea that you do not know anything. You have evolved so far that this ignorance is actually a pleasure because it leaves you open to constantly expanding your perception. It's like a dance, at the same time solidified and open. It is really an interesting dance, because it is a skill. Anyone can learn a skill, but this type of skill is very hard to learn because it is so contrary to our usual way of thinking. You must know that you basically know nothing and be satisfied with it. That way, you always stay open to the mystery. In my opinion, that's what every good spiritual path should teach.[1]

---

[1] Kalisch, Sven, Religion und Gewissheit. Anmerkungen zu einem epistemologischen Problem und eine schamanische Lösung. In: Werbick, Jürgen, Kalisch, Muhammad Sven, and von Stosch, Klaus (eds.), *Verwundete Gewissheit. Strategien zum Umgang mit Verunsicherung in Islam und Christentum.* Paderborn u. a. 2010, 31–52, 51.

Bibliography

Abū-Zaid, Naṣr Ḥāmid, *Gottes Menschenwort. Für ein humanistisches Verständnis des Koran.* Freiburg i. Br. 2008.
Aren, Edmund, *Gottesverständigung: Eine kommunikative Religionstheologie.* Freiburg i. Br. 2007.
Arendt, Hannah, *Eichmann in Jerusalem. Ein Bericht von der Banalität des Bösen.* Munich 2011.
Asad, Muhammad, *The Message of the Qur'an.* Bristol 2003.
Aslan, Ednan, Situation und Strömungen der islamischen Religionspädagogik im deutschsprachigen Raum. In: *Theo-Web. Zeitschrift für Religionspädagogik* (2012) 11, 10–18.
Aslan, Ednan, 'Wir erwarten europaweit Impulse'. Die Stimme eines Hochschullehrers. In: Behr, Harry Harun, Rohe, Mathias, and Schmid, Hansjörg (eds.), *'Den Koran zu lesen genügt nicht!'. Fachliches Profil und realer Kontext für ein neues Berufsfeld. Auf dem Weg zum Islamischen Religionsunterricht.* Berlin 2008, 63–74.
Assmann, Jan, *Monotheismus und die Sprache der Gewalt.* Vienna 2009.
Baier, Karl, Spiritualität und Identität. In: Bernhardt, Reinhold, and Schmidt-Leukel, Perry (eds.), *Multiple religiöse Identität. Aus verschiedenen religiösen Traditionen schöpfen.* Zurich 2008, 187–218.
Baier, Karl, Transreligiöse Theorie und existentiale Interpretation. Internet resource: <https://homepage.univie.ac.at/karl.baier/texte/pdf/Transreligioese Theorie.pdf> [accessed on February 17, 2017].
Bauer, Thomas, *Die Kultur der Ambiguität. Eine andere Geschichte des Islams.* Berlin 2011.
Behr, Harry Harun, Bildungstheoretisches Nachdenken als Grundlage für eine islamische Religionsdidaktik. In: Kaddor, Lamya (ed.), *Islamische Erziehungs- und Bildungslehre.* Berlin 2008, 49–65.
Behr, Harry Harun, *Islamische Bildungslehre.* Garching 1998.
Bernhardt, Reinhold, 'Synkretismus' als Deutekategorie für multireligiöse Identitätsbildungen. In: Bernhardt, Reinhold, and Schmidt-Leukel, Perry (eds.), *Multiple religiöse Identität. Aus verschiedenen religiösen Traditionen schöpfen.* Zurich 2008, 267–290.
Bhabha, Homi K., *Die Verortung der Kultur.* Tübingen 2000.

Bielefeldt, Heiner, *Menschenrechte in der Einwanderungsgesellschaft. Plädoyer für einen aufgeklärten Multikulturalismus*. Bielefeld 2015.

Bielefeldt, Heiner, *Muslime im säkularen Rechtsstaat. Integrationschancen durch Religionsfreiheit*. Bielefeld 2003.

Bielefeldt, Heiner, Muslimische Minderheiten im säkularen Rechtsstaat. In: Bukow, Wolf-Dietrich, and Yildriz, Erol (eds.), *Islam und Bildung* (Interkulturelle Studien, Vol. 15). Opladen 2003, 21–36.

Bilgin, Beyza, *Egitim Bilimi ve Din Egitimi*. Ankara 1988.

Bobzin, Hartmut (ed.), *Der Koran. In der Übersetzung von Friedrich Rückert*. Würzburg 2002.

Bozkurt, Nebi, Medrese. In: Türkiye Diyanet vakfi (ed.), *İslâm ansiklopedisi. Standardausgabe*. İstanbul 1988.

Bukow, Wolf-Dietrich, Der Islam – ein bildungspolitisches Thema. In: Bukow, Wolf-Dietrich, and Yildiz, Erol (eds.), *Islam und Bildung* (Interkulturelle Studien, Vol. 15). Opladen 2003, 57–80.

Casanova, José, *Europas Angst vor der Religion*. Berlin 2009.

Cohn, Ruth C., From Couch to circle to community. Beginnings of the Theme-Centered Interactional Method. In: Ruitenbeek, Hendrik Marinus (ed.), *Group Therapy Today*. New York 1969, 256–267.

Cohn, Ruth C., 'Sich zur eigenen Autorität und Fehlbarkeit bekennen.' Gesprächspartner: Albert Biesinger and Thomas Schreijäck (1985). In: Cohn, Ruth C., *Es geht ums Anteilnehmen ... Perspektiven der Persönlichkeitsentfaltung in der Gesellschaft der Jahrtausendwende*. Freiburg i. Br. 1989, 127–141.

Cohn, Ruth C., *Von der Psychoanalyse zur themenzentrierten Interaktion. Von der Behandlung einzelner zu einer Pädagogik für alle*. Stuttgart 2009.

Cohn, Ruth C., 'Zuwenig geben ist Diebstahl – zuviel geben ist Mord!' Gesprächspartner: Otto Herz (1981). In: Cohn, Ruth C., *Es geht ums Anteilnehmen ... Perspektiven der Persönlichkeitsentfaltung in der Gesellschaft der Jahrtausendwende*. Freiburg i. Br. 1989, 142–152.

Cohn, Ruth C., and Farau, Alfred, *Gelebte Geschichte der Psychotherapie. Zwei Perspektiven*. Stuttgart 2008.

Cragg, Kenneth, *The Privilege of Man. A theme in Judaism, Islam and Christianity*. London 1968.

Dalferth, Ingolf U., Religionsfixierte Moderne? Der lange Weg vom säkularen Zeitalter zur post-säkularen Welt. In: *Denkströme. Journal der Sächsischen Akademie der Wissenschaften* (2011) 7, 9–32.

Ebert, Hans-Georg (ed.), *Der Islam und die Grundlagen der Herrschaft. Übersetzung und Kommentar des Werkes von Alî Abd ar-Râziq*. Frankfurt a. M. 2010.

Egan, Kieran, *Teaching as story telling. An alternative approach to teaching and the curriculum*. Chicago 1989.

Ellis, Gail, and Brewster, Jean, *Tell it again! - The new storytelling handbook for primary teachers*. Harlow 2002.
Engel, Christine, and Lewicki, Roman, Vorwort Konzepte der Interkulturalität. In: Engel, Christine, and Lewicki, Roman (eds.), *Interkulturalität. Slawistische Fallstudien*. Innsbruck 2005, 9–19.
Engel, Manfred (ed.), *Rilke–Handbuch. Leben – Werk – Wirkung*. Stuttgart 2004.
Englert, Rudolf, Bildungsstandards für Religion. Was eigentlich wissen sollte, wer solche formulieren wollte. In: Sajak, Clauß Peter (ed.), *Bildungsstandards für den Religionsunterricht*. Berlin 2007, 9–28.
Englert, Rudolf, *Religionspädagogische Grundfragen. Anstöße zur Urteilsbildung*. Stuttgart 2007.
Faber, Roland, Der transreligiöse Diskurs. In: *Polylog. Zeitschrift für interkulturelles Philosophieren* (2003) 9, 65–94.
Faßhauer, Uwe, 1. Axiom: existentiell-anthropologisches Axiom. In: Schneider-Landolf, Mina, Spielmann, Jochen, and Zitterbarth, Walter (eds.), *Handbuch Themenzentrierte Interaktion (TZI)*. Göttingen 2009, 80–85.
Forschungskreis Kommunikative Theologie/Communicative Theology Research Group (ed.), *Kommunikative Theologie. Selbstvergewisserung unserer Kultur des Theologietreibens/Communicative Theology. Reflections on the Culture of Our Practice of Theology* (Kommunikative Theologie – interdisziplinär/Communicative Theology – Interdisciplinary Studies, Vol. 1). Vienna 2007.
Frickel, Michael, Von der TZI zur themenzentrierte Meditation. Grund und Ziel einer Änderung. In: Löhmer, Cornelia, and Standhardt, Rüdiger (eds.), *TZI. Pädagogisch-therapeutische Gruppenarbeit nach Ruth C. Cohn*. Stuttgart 1992, 218–229.
Fuchs, Martin, Das Ende der Modelle: Interkulturalität statt (Kultur-)Vergleich. Cited in: Holzinger, Markus, *Kontingenz der Gegenwartsgesellschaft. Dimensionen eines Leitbegriffs moderner Sozialtheorie*. Bielefeld 2007.
Funke, Dieter, *Verkündigung zwischen Tradition und Interaktion. Praktisch-theologische Studien zur Themenzentrierten Interaktion (TZI) nach Ruth C. Cohn*. Frankfurt a. M. 1984.
Grimmitt, Michael, When is 'Commitment' a Problem in Religious Education? In: *British Journal of Educational Studies* (1981) 29, 42–53.
Günther, Sebastian, Bildungsauffassungen klassischer muslimischer Gelehrter. Von Abu Hanifa bis Ibn Khaldun (8. –15. Jh.). In: Sejdini, Zekirija (ed.), *Islamische Theologie und Religionspädagogik in Bewegung. Neue Ansätze in Europa*. Bielefeld 2016, 51–71.
Günther, Sebastian, Das Buch ist ein Gefäß gefüllt mit Wissen und Scharfsinn. In: Gemeinhardt, Peter, and Günther, Sebastian (eds.), *Von Rom nach Bagdad.*

Bildung und Religion von der römischen Kaiserzeit bis zum klassischen Islam. Tübingen 2013, 357–379.

Habermas, Jürgen, *Erkenntnis und Interesse. Mit einem neuen Nachwort*. Frankfurt a. M. 2001.

Hagleitner, Silvia, *Mit Lust an der Welt – in Sorge um sie. Feministisch-politische Bildungsarbeit nach Paulo Freire und Ruth C. Cohn*. Mainz 1996.

Hajatpour, Reza, Mensch und Gott. Von islamisch-philosophischen Menschenbildern. In: Behr, Harry Harun, and Ulfat, Fahimah (eds.), *Zwischen Himmel und Erde. Bildungsphilosophische Verhältnisbestimmungen von Heiligem Text und Geist*. Münster 2014, 77–90.

Halbmayr, Alois, and Hafner Johann, *Negative Theologie heute? Zum aktuellen Stellenwert einer umstrittenen Tradition*. Freiburg i. Br. 2008.

Hilberath, Bernd Jochen, and Scharer, Matthias, *Kommunikative Theologie. Grundlagen – Erfahrungen – Klärungen* (Kommunikative Theologie 15). Ostfildern 2013.

Höhn, Hans-Joachim, Reflexive Modernisierung – reflexive Säkularisierung. In: Gmainer-Pranzl, Franz, and Rettenbacher, Sigrid (eds.), *Religion in postsäkularer Gesellschaft. Interdisziplinäre Perspektiven* (Salzburger interdisziplinäre Diskurse, Vol. 3). Frankfurt a. M. 2013, 15–34.

Holzinger, Markus, *Kontingenz der Gegenwartsgesellschaft. Dimensionen eines Leitbegriffs moderner Sozialtheorie*. Bielefeld 2007.

Honsel, Bernhard, *Der rote Punkt. Eine Gemeinde unterwegs*. Düsseldorf 1985.

Hünermann, Peter, *Die Dokumente des Zweiten Vatikanischen Konzils. Konstitutionen, Dekrete, Erklärungen*. Darmstadt 2012.

Ibn Rushd, *Maßgebliche Abhandlung. Faṣl al-maqāl*. Berlin 2010.

Insam, Heribert, Lieber mutig statt ängstlich. In: *Tiroler Tageszeitung*, January 6, 2017, 4f.

Juen, Maria, *Die ersten Minuten des Unterrichts. Skizzen einer Kairologie des Anfangs aus kommunikativ-theologischer Perspektive*. Münster 2013.

Juen, Maria, et al. (eds.), *Anders gemeinsam – gemeinsam anders? In Ambivalenzen lebendig kommunizieren* (Kommunikative Theologie, Vol. 18). Mainz 2015.

Kalisch, Sven, Religion und Gewissheit. Anmerkungen zu einem epistemologischen Problem und eine schamanische Lösung. In: Werbick, Jürgen, Kalisch, Muhammad Sven, and von Stosch, Klaus (eds.), *Verwundete Gewissheit. Strategien zum Umgang mit Verunsicherung in Islam und Christentum*. Paderborn 2010, 31–52.

Kalsky, Manuela, Religiöse Flexibilität. Eine Antwort auf kulturelle und religiöse Vielfalt. In: Bernhardt, Reinhold, and Schmidt-Leukel, Perry (eds.), *Multiple religiöse Identität. Aus verschiedenen religiösen Traditionen schöpfen*. Zurich 2008, 219–242.

Karimi, Ahmad Milad, Wahrheit ist Sehnsucht. 'So wetteifert um die guten Dinge.' In: Langthaler, Rudolf, and Tück, Jan Heiner (eds.), *'Es strebe von euch jeder um die Wette.' Lessings Ringparabel – ein Paradigma für die Verständigung der Religionen heute?* Freiburg i. Br. 2016, 278–292.

Kästle, Daniela, Kraml, Martina, and Mohagheghi, Hamideh (eds.), *Heilig-Tabu. Christen und Muslime wagen Begegnungen* (Kommunikative Theologie, Vol. 13). Ostfildern 2009.

Kelpetin, Hatice, İlmihal. In: Türkiye Diyanet vakfi (ed.), *İslâm ansiklopedisi. Standardausgabe.* Istanbul 1988, 139–141.

Khorchide, Mouhanad, *Islam der Barmherzigkeit. Grundzüge einer modernen Religion* (Herder Spektrum, Vol. 6764). Freiburg i. Br. 2015.

Khoury, Adel Theodor (trans.), *Der Koran.* Band 1. Sure 1,1–2,74. Gütersloh 1990.

Kirchenamt der Evangelischen Kirche in Deutschland (ed.), *Klarheit und gute Nachbarschaft. Christen und Muslime in Deutschland.* Hannover 2006.

Kokemohr, Rainer, Bildung als Welt- und Selbstentwurf im Anspruch des Fremden. In: Koller, Hans-Christoph, Marotzki, Winfried, and Sanders, Olaf (eds.), *Bildungsprozesse und Fremdheitserfahrung. Beiträge zu einer Theorie transformatorischer Bildungsprozesse.* Bielefeld 2007, 13–68.

Kraml, Martina, *Dissertation gestalten im Raum der Möglichkeiten. Eine theologiedidaktische Studie zu Dissertationsprozessen mit besonderer Aufmerksamkeit auf die Entwicklung empirischer Forschung,* unveröffentlichte Habilitationsschrift. Innsbruck 2013.

Kraml, Martina, Grenzgänge. In: Scharer, Matthias, and Kraml, Martina (eds.), *Vom Leben herausgefordert. Praktisch-theologisches Forschen als kommunikativer Prozess.* Mainz 2003, 159–179.

Kraml, Martina, The published word is not the final one … Kontingenzsensible theologische Forschung auf dem Hintergrund des Forschungsprogrammes Kommunikative Theologie. In: *Zeitschrift für katholische Theologie* (2014) 136, 233–250.

Kraml, Martina, Sejdini, Zekirija, Bauer, Nicole, and Kolb, Jonas, *Konflikte und Konfliktpotentiale in interreligiösen Bildungsprozessen. Empirisch begleitete Grenzgänge zwischen Schule und Universität* (Studien zur Interreligiösen Religionspädagogik, Vol. 3). Stuttgart 2020.

Kraml, Martina, and Sejdini, Zekirija (eds.), *Interreligiöse Bildungsprozesse. Empirische Einblicke in Schul- und Hochschulkontexte* (Studien zur Interreligiösen Religionspädagogik, Vol. 2). Stuttgart 2018.

Kroeger, Matthias, Das sogenannte Störungspostulat: 'Disturbances and passionate involvements take precedence.' In: von Kanitz, Anja et al. (eds.), *Elemente der Themenzentrierten Interaktion. Texte zur Aus- und Weiterbildung.* Göttingen 2015, 132–144.

Kroeger, Matthias, *Themenzentrierte Seelsorge. Über die Kombination klientenzentrierter und themenzentrierter Arbeit nach Carl R. Rogers und Ruth C. Cohn in Theologie und schulischer Gruppenarbeit*. Stuttgart 1989.

Kropač, Ulrich, Religiöse Pluralität als religionspädagogische Herausforderung. Perspektiven interreligiösen Lernens. In: Böttigheimer, Christoph, and Filser, Hubert (eds.), *Kircheneinheit und Weltverantwortung. Festschrift für Peter Neuner*. Regensburg 2006, 471–486.

Lahbabi, Mohammed Aziz, *Der Mensch: Zeuge Gottes. Entwurf einer islamischen Anthropologie*. Freiburg i. Br. 2011.

Lakoff, George, and Wehling, Elisabeth, *Auf leisen Sohlen ins Gehirn. Politische Sprache und ihre heimliche Macht*. Heidelberg 2008.

Langmaack, Barbara, *Einführung in die Themenzentrierte Interaktion TZI. Leben rund ums Dreieck*. Weinheim 2001.

Largen Johnson, Kristin, *Finding God Among Our Neighbours. An Interfaith Systematic Theology*. Minneapolis, MN 2013.

Lederer, Bernd, *Kompetenz oder Bildung? Eine Analyse jüngerer Konnotationsverschiebungen des Bildungsbegriffs und Plädoyer für eine Rück- und Neubesinnung auf ein transinstrumentelles Bildungsverständnis*. Innsbruck 2012.

Leimgruber, Stephan, *Interreligiöses Lernen*. Munich 2007.

Liessmann, Konrad Paul, *Geisterstunde. Die Praxis der Unbildung. Eine Streitschrift*. Vienna 2014.

Lingen-Ali, Ulrike, and Mecheril, Paul, Religion als soziale Deutungspraxis. In: *Österreichisches Religionspädagogisches Forum* (2016) 2, 17–24.

Lübbe, Hermann, *Religion nach der Aufklärung*. Graz 1990.

Luther, Henning, *Religion und Alltag. Bausteine einer Praktischen Theologie des Subjekts*, Stuttgart 1992.

Masschelein, Jan, and Simsons, Maarten, *Globale Immunität. Oder eine kleine Kartographie des europäischen Bildungsraums*. Zurich 2012.

Mecheril, Paul, 'Kompetenzlosigkeitskompetenz'. Pädagogisches Handeln unter Einwanderungsbedingungen. In: Auernheimer, Georg (ed.), *Interkulturelle Kompetenz und pädagogische Professionalität*. Wiesbaden 2010, 15–34.

Meyer-Drawe, Käte, 'Du sollst dir kein Bildnis noch Gleichnis machen …' – Bildung und Versagung. In: Koller, Hans-Christoph, Marotzki, Winfried, and Sanders, Olaf (eds.), *Bildungsprozesse und Fremdheitserfahrung. Beiträge zu einer Theorie transformatorischer Bildungsprozesse*. Bielefeld 2007, 83–94.

Meyer-Drawe, Käte, Entbildung – Einbildung – Bildung. Zur Bedeutung der Imago-Die-Lehre für moderne Bildungstheorien. In: Behrens, Rudolf (ed.), *Ordnungen des Imaginären. Theorien der Imagination in funktionsgeschichtlicher Zeit*. Hamburg 2001, 181–194.

Müller, Rabeya, Islamische Perspektiven zum interreligiösen Lernen: Wie 'inter-' ist der Islam? In: Schreiner, Peter (ed.), *Handbuch interreligiöses Lernen*. Gütersloh 2005, 142–149.

Musil, Robert, *Der Mann ohne Eigenschaften I. Erstes und zweites Buch*. Reinbeck bei Hamburg 1987.

Nassehi, Armin, and Saake, Irmhild, Kontingenz: Methodisch verhindert oder beobachtet? In: *Zeitschrift für Soziologie* (2002) 1, 66–86.

Nausner, Michael, Heimat als Grenzland. Territorien christlicher Subjektivität. In: Nehring, Andreas, and Tielesch, Simon (eds.), *Postkoloniale Theologien. Bibelhermeneutische und kulturwissenschaftliche Beiträge*. Stuttgart 2013, 187–202.

Nitsche, Bernhard, and Panikkar, Raimon, Multiple Identität als gelebte inter-intrareligiöse Transversalität. In: Bernhardt, Reinhold, and Schmidt-Leukel, Perry (eds.), *Multiple Identität. Aus verschiedenen religiösen Quellen schöpfen*. Zurich 2008, 59–78.

Nussbaum, Martha, *Die neue Intoleranz. Ein Ausweg der Politik aus der Angst*. Darmstadt 2014.

Ockel, Anita, and Cohn, Ruth C., Das Konzept des Widerstands in der themenzentrierten Interaktion. Vom psychoanalytischen Konzept des Widerstandes über das TZI-Konzept der Störung zum Ansatz einer Gesellschaftstherapie. In: Löhmer, Cornelia, and Standhardt, Rüdiger (eds.), *TZI. Pädagogisch-therapeutische Gruppenarbeit nach Ruth C. Cohn*. Stuttgart 1992, 177–206.

Ostertag, Margit, Von Ruth Cohn und Paulo Freire lernen. Annäherungen an eine bildungstheoretisch fundierte Hochschuldidaktik. In: Miller, Tilly, and Ostertag, Margit (eds.), *Hochschulbildung. Wiederaneignung eines existentiell bedeutsamen Begriffs*. Berlin 2017, 123–133.

Palaver, Wolfgang, Christentum im säkularen Kontext. Grenzen und Chancen. In: Kästle, Daniela, Kraml, Martina, and Mohagheghi, Hamideh (eds.), *Heilig-Tabu. Christen und Muslime wagen Begegnungen* (Kommunikative Theologie, Vol. 13). Ostfildern 2009, 311–318.

Panhofer, Johannes, Eintauchen in die 'interreligiöse Lebenswelt'. Methodisch geleitete Erkundungen im Dialogprozess der Jännertagung. In: Kästle, Daniela, Kraml, Martina, and Mohagheghi, Hamideh (eds.), *Heilig-Tabu. Christen und Muslime wagen Begegnungen* (Kommunikative Theologie, Vol. 13). Ostfildern 2009, 107–119.

Pope Francis, Ansprache von Papst Franziskus an den Europarat. Straßburg, Frankreich Dienstag, 25. November 2014. Internet resource: <https://w2.vatican.va/content/francesco/de/speeches/2014/november/documents/papa-francesco_20141125_strasburgo-consiglio-europa.html> [accessed on February 10, 2017].

Peter, Teresa, 'Ich stehe vor Dir.' Die Bedeutung von spirituellem Anteil-nehmen-Lassen und Anteil-Nehmen im Dialog. In: Kästle, Kraml and Mohagheghi (eds.), *Heilig-Tabu. Christen und Muslime wagen Begegnungen* (Kommunikative Theologie, Vol. 13). Ostfildern 2009, 215–220.

Pieper, Annemarie, Riskante Freiheit. Der Hang zum Bösen und seine Folgen. In: Lindenau, Mathias, and Meier Kressig, Marcel (eds.), *Was ist der Mensch? Vier ethische Betrachtungen* (Vadian Lectures, Vol. 1). Bielefeld 2015, 51–70.

Pirker, Viera, Lernen mit der eigenen Biografie in der Religionslehrerbildung. Theoretische Aspekte. In: *Religionspädagogische Beiträge. Zeitschrift der Arbeitsgemeinschaft Katholische Religionspädagogik und Katechetik* (2016) 74, 56–67.

Rahner, Karl, *Hörer des Wortes. Zur Grundlegung einer Religionsphilosophie*. Freiburg i. Br. 1971.

Reiser, Helmut, Vorschlag für eine theoretische Grundlegung der Themenzentrierten Interaktion. In: *Themenzentrierte Interaktion. Theme-centered interaction* (2014) 2, 69–77.

Renn, Joachim, and Straub, Jürgen, Der Prozesscharakter moderner personaler Selbstverhältnisse. In: Straub, Jürgen, and Renn, Joachim (eds.), *Transitorische Identität. Der Prozesscharakter des modernen Selbst*. Frankfurt a. Main 2002, 10–31.

Renz, Andreas, *Der Mensch unter dem An-Spruch Gottes. Offenbarungsverständnis und Menschenbild des Islam im Urteil gegenwärtiger christlicher Theologie* (Christentum und Islam, Vol. 1). Würzburg 2002.

Renz, Andreas, Die 'Zeichen Gottes' (ayat Allah). Sakramentalität im Islam und ihre Bedeutung für das christlich-islamische Verhältnis. In: *Theologische Zeitschrift* (2005), 239–257.

Rickers, Folkert, Interreligiöses Lernen. In: Mette, Robert, and Rickers, Folkert (eds.), *Lexikon der Religionspädagogik*. Neukirchen-Vluyn 2001, 874–881.

Rose, Nadine, 'Für 'nen Ausländer gar nicht mal schlecht'. Zur Interpretation von Subjektbildungsprozessen in Migrationsbiographien. In: Mecheril, Paul (ed.), *Subjektbildung. Interdisziplinäre Analysen der Migrationsgesellschaft*. Bielefeld 2014, 57–77.

Röttgers, Kurt, *Identität als Ereignis. Zur Neufindung eines Begriffs*. Bielefeld 2016.

Rubner, Angelika, and Rubner, Eike, *Unterwegs zur funktionierenden Gruppe. Die Gestaltung von Gruppenprozessen mit der Themenzentrierten Interaktion*. Gießen 2016.

Saake, Irmhild, Selbstbeschreibungen als Weltbeschreibungen. Die Homologie-Annahme revisited. In: *Sociologia Internationalis. Europäische Zeitschrift für Kulturforschung* (2005) 1/2, 99–139.

Sarikaya, Yasar, Wege zu einer Islamischen Religionspädagogik in Deutschland. In: Ucar, Bülent, Blasberg-Kuhnke, Martina, and Scheliha, Arnulf von (eds.), *Religionen in der Schule und die Bedeutung des Islamischen Religionsunterrichts*. Göttingen 2010, 191–199.

Schambeck, Mirjam, *Interreligiöse Kompetenz. Basiswissen für Studium, Ausbildung und Beruf*. Göttingen 2013.

Schambeck, Mirjam, 'Weil es um den Menschen geht, wenn wir von Bildung reden ...' – Religionspädagogische Einmischungen zur Debatte um Bildungsstandards. In: Sajak, Clauß Peter (ed.), *Bildungsstandards für den Religionsunterricht*. Berlin 2007, 179–202.

Scharer, Matthias, Die Schule und das Leben (in Fülle). Religionspädagogische Optionen in der Schulentwicklung. In: Jäggle, Martin, Krobath, Thomas, and Schelander, Robert (eds.), *lebens.werte.schule. Religiöse Dimensionen in Schulkultur und Schulentwicklung*. Vienna 2009, 379–386.

Scharer, Matthias, Learning (in/through) Religion in the Presence of the Other. Accident and/or Test Case in Public Education? In: Juen, Maria, et al. (eds.), *Anders gemeinsam – gemeinsam anders? In Ambivalenzen lebendig kommunizieren* (Kommunikative Theologie, Vol. 18). Mainz 2015, 223–238.

Scharer, Matthias, Lebendigen Lernprozessen trauen, Kompetenzen fördern. Das 'Innsbrucker Modell' der ReligionslehrerInnenausbildung unter der Herausforderung des Kompetenz- und Standarddiskurses in der Religionsdidaktik. In: *Österreichisches Religionspädagogisches Forum* (2013) 1, 58–63.

Scharer, Matthias, Religion unterrichten lernen. Das Innsbrucker Modell. In: Arntz, Anne, and Isenberg, Wolfgang (eds.), *Kompetenz für die Praxis? Innovative Modelle der Religionslehreraus- und -fortbildung*. Bergisch. Gladbach 2000, 55–68.

Scharer, Matthias, 'Third Spaces' – Räume für interreligiöse Begegnung an 'Generativen' Themen. In: Datterl, Monika, Guggenberger, Wilhelm, and Paganini, Claudia (eds.), *Gewalt im Namen Gottes – ein bleibendes Problem?* Innsbruck 2016, 71–90.

Scharer, Matthias, TZI in der kirchlichen Praxis. In: Löhmer, Cornelia, and Standhardt, Rüdiger (eds.), *TZI. Pädagogisch-therapeutische Gruppenarbeit nach Ruth C. Cohn*. Stuttgart 1992, 312–325.

Scharer, Matthias, and Hilberath, Bernd Jochen (eds.), *The practice of Communicative Theology. Introduction to a new theological culture*. New York 2008.

Schärtl, Thomas, *Wahrheit und Gewissheit. Zur Eigenart religiösen Glaubens*. Kevelaer 2004.

Schellenberg, Annette, Vernunft/Verstand (AT). Internet resource: <https://www.bibelwissenschaft.de/stichwort/34095/> [accessed on January 30, 2017].

Schimmel, Annemarie, *Die Zeichen Gottes. Die religiöse Welt des Islam*. Munich 1995.
Schneider-Landolf, Mina, Spielmann, Jochen, and Zitterbarth, Walter (eds.), *Handbuch Themenzentrierte Interaktion (TZI)*. Göttingen 2009.
Schoeler, Gregor, Gesprochenes Wort und Schrift. Mündlichkeit und Schriftlichkeit im frühislamischen Lehrbetrieb. In: Gemeinhardt, Peter, and Günther, Sebastian (eds.), *Von Rom nach Bagdad. Bildung und Religion von der römischen Kaiserzeit bis zum klassischen Islam*. Tübingen 2013, 269–289.
Schratz, Michael, Schwarz, Johanna, and Westfall-Greiter, Tanja, *Lernen als bildende Erfahrung. Vignetten in der Praxisforschung*. Innsbruck 2012.
Schulamt der Diözese Innsbruck (ed.), *Miteinander Feiern in der Schule. (Religiöse) Feiern im multireligiösen Schulkontext*. September 2016.
Schweitzer, Friedrich, *Interreligiöse Bildung. Religiöse Vielfalt als religionspädagogische Herausforderung und Chance*. Munich 2014.
Seckler, Max, *Die schiefen Wände des Lehrhauses*. Freiburg i. Br. 1988.
Sejdini, Zekirija, Armutsbekämpfung und Gerechtigkeit aus islamischer Perspektive. In: Ströbele, Christian et al. (eds.), *Armut und Gerechtigkeit. Christliche und islamische Perspektiven*. Regensburg 2016, 295–300.
Sejdini, Zekirija, Grundlagen eines theologiesensiblen und beteiligtenbezogenen Modells islamischer Religionspädagogik und Religionsdidaktik im deutschsprachigen Kontext. In: *Österreichisches Religionspädagogisches Forum* (2015) 1, 21–28.
Sejdini, Zekirija, Interreligiöser Dialog aus muslimischer Perspektive. In: Gmainer-Pranz, Franz, Ingruber, Astrit, and Ladstätter, Markus (eds.), '*... mit Klugheit und Liebe'. Dokumentation der Tagung zur Förderung des interreligiösen Dialogs 2012–2015*. Linz 2017, 241–251.
Sejdini, Zekirija, Zwischen Gewissheit und Kontingenz. Auf dem Weg zu einem neuen Verständnis von islamischer Theologie und Religionspädagogik im europäischen Kontext. In: Sejdini, Zekirija (ed.), *Islamische Theologie und Religionspädagogik in Bewegung. Neue Ansätze in Europa*. Bielefeld 2016, 15–31.
Sejdini, Zekirija, Kraml, Martina, and Scharer, Matthias, *Mensch werden. Grundlagen einer interreligiösen Religionspädagogik und -didaktik aus muslimisch-christlicher Perspektive* (Studien zur Interreligiösen Religionspädagogik, Vol. 1). Stuttgart 2017.
Sejdini, Zekirija (ed.), *Islamische Theologie und Religionspädagogik in Bewegung. Neue Ansätze in Europa*. Bielefeld 2016.
Sekretariat der Deutschen Bischofskonferenz (ed.), *Leitlinien für das Gebet bei Treffen von Christen, Juden und Muslimen. Eine Handreichung der deutschen Bischöfe*. Bonn 2008.
Siebenrock, Roman A. (ed.), *Handeln Gottes. Beiträge zur aktuellen Debatte*. Freiburg i. Br. 2014.

Simon, Fritz, *Die Kunst, nicht zu lernen und andere Paradoxien in Psychotherapie, Management, Politik*. Heidelberg 1999.
Stollberg, Dietrich, *Lernen, weil es Freude macht. Eine Einführung in die Themenzentrierte Interaktion*. Munich 1982.
von Stosch, Klaus, Was sind religiöse Überzeugungen? In: Joas, Hans (ed.), *Was sind religiöse Überzeugungen?* Göttingen 2003, 103–146.
Taylor, Charles, *Ein säkulares Zeitalter*. Frankfurt a. M. 2012.
Thurner, Martin, Von der Information zur Kommunikation. Das Offenbarungs verständnis der beiden Vatikanischen Konzilien. In: Heinzmann, Richard, and Selçuk, Mualla (eds.), *Offenbarung in Christentum und Islam* (Interkulturelle und interreligiöse Symposien der Eugen-Biser-Stiftung, Vol. 5). Stuttgart 2011, 129–143.
Tietze, Nikola, Muslimische Identitäten. In: Bukow, Wolf-Dietrich, and Yildiz, Erol (eds.), *Islam und Bildung* (Interkulturelle Studien, Vol. 15). Opladen 2003, 83–91.
Ucar, Bülent, Islamische Religionspädagogik im deutschen Kontext. Die Neukonstituierung eines alten Faches unter veränderten Rahmenbedingungen. In: Ucar, Bülent, Blasberg-Kuhnke, Martina, and Scheliha, Arnulf von (eds.), *Religionen in der Schule und die Bedeutung des Islamischen Religionsunterrichts*. Göttingen 2010, 33–49.
Ucar, Bülent, Synopse für das Fach 'Islamunterricht' in der Grundschule: Zwischen didaktischem Profil und inhaltlicher Gestaltung. In: Kiefer, Michael, Gottwald, Eckart, and Ucar, Bülent (eds.), *Auf dem Weg zum islamischen Religionsunterricht. Sachstand und Perspektiven in Nordrhein-Westfalen*. Berlin 2008, 121–140.
Vogt, Peter, *Kontingenz und Zufall. Eine Ideen- und Begriffsgeschichte*, Berlin 2011.
Welsch, Wolfgang, 'Was ist eigentlich Transkulturalität'. In: Darowska, Lucyna, Lüttenberg, Thomas, and Machold, Claudia (eds.), *Hochschule als transkultureller Raum? Kultur, Bildung und Differenz in der Universität*, Bielefeld 2010, 39–66.
Werbick, Jürgen, *Glaubenlernen aus Erfahrung. Grundbegriffe einer Didaktik des Glaubens*. Munich 1989.
Werner, Gunda, *Macht Glaube glücklich? Freiheit und Bezogenheit als Erfahrung persönlicher Heilszusage*. Regensburg 2005.
Wielandt, Rotraud, Der Mensch und seine Stellung in der Schöpfung. Zum Grundverständnis islamischer Anthropologie. In: Bsteh, Andreas, and Hagemann, Ludwig (eds.), *Der Islam als Anfrage an christliche Theologie und Philosophie. Referate – Anfragen – Diskussionen* (Christentum in der Begegnung). Mödling 1994, 97–105.

Wielandt, Rotraud, *Offenbarung und Geschichte im Denken moderner Muslime*. Wiesbaden 1971.

Willems, Joachim, *Interreligiöse Kompetenz. Theoretische Grundlagen – Konzeptualisierungen – Unterrichtsmethoden*. Wiesbaden 2011.

Wissenschaftsrat, Empfehlungen zur Weiterentwicklung von Theologien und religionsbezogenen Wissenschaften an deutschen Hochschulen. <http://www.wissenschaftsrat.de/download/archiv/9678-10.pdf> [accessed on February 15, 2017].

Wuchterl, Kurt, *Kontingenz oder das Andere der Vernunft. Zum Verhältnis von Philosophie, Naturwissenschaft und Religion*. Stuttgart 2011.

Wulf, Christoph, and Zirfass, Jörg, Homo educandus. Eine Einleitung in die Pädagogische Anthropologie. In: Wulf, Christoph, and Zirfass, Jörg (eds.), *Handbuch pädagogischer Anthropologie*. Wiesbaden 2014, 9–26.

Yildiz, Erol, Postmigrantische Perspektiven. Von der Hegemonie zur urbanen Alltagspraxis. In: Doğmuş, Aysun, Karakaşoğlu, Yasemin, and Mecheril, Paul (eds.), *Pädagogisches Können in der Migrationsgesellschaft*. Wiesbaden 2016, 71–82.

Yildiz, Safiye, *Interkulturelle Erziehung und Pädagogik. Subjektivierung und Macht in den Ordnungen des nationalen Diskurses*, Wiesbaden 2009.

Ziebertz, Hans-Georg, Der Beitrag der christlichen Theologie zur Imameausbildung. In: Ucar, Bülent (ed.), *Imamausbildung in Deutschland. Islamische Theologie im europäischen Kontext* (Veröffentlichungen des Zentrums für Interkulturelle Islamstudien der Universität Osnabrück, Vol. 3). Göttingen 2010, 289–305.

Ziebertz, Hans-Georg, Religionspädagogik und empirische Methodologie. In: Schweitzer, Friedrich, and Schlag, Thomas (eds.), *Religionspädagogik im 21. Jahrhundert. Herausforderungen und Zukunftsperspektiven*. Gütersloh/Freiburg i. Br., 209–222.

Zweites Vatikanisches Konzil, *Dogmatische Konstitution über die göttliche Offenbarung Dei Verbum*, Nr. 2.

Zweites Vatikanisches Konzil, *Pastorale Konstitution über die Kirche in der Welt von heute Gaudium et spes*, Nr. 4.

www.ingramcontent.com/pod-product-compliance
Lightning Source LLC
Chambersburg PA
CBHW050123020526
44112CB00035B/2363